THE TEENAGE YEARS

MARIE MURRAY

COLM KEANE

Published in association with
RADIO TELEFÍS ÉIREANN

MERCIER PRESS

MERCIER PRESS
PO Box 5, 5 French Church Street, Cork
and
16 Hume Street, Dublin

Trade enquiries to CMD DISTRIBUTION,
55a Spruce Avenue, Stillorgan Industrial Park, Blackrock, Dublin

© Marie Murray & Colm Keane, 1997

ISBN 1 85635 195 5

.   10 9 8 7 6 5 4 3 2 1

A CIP record for this book is available from the British Library.

Printed in Ireland by Colour Books Ltd.

CONTENTS

ACKNOWLEDGEMENTS

There are many people to be thanked for their help in compiling this book. The authors would particularly like to mention Karen Murray and Aisling Murray for their advice and direction. Thanks also to Úna O'Hagan and Seán Keane for their sustained encouragement and support.

Particular mention must also be made of all the staff at St Vincent's Psychiatric Hospital, Dublin and St Joseph's Adolescent Services, Dublin, especially Edward Byrne, Dr Nuala Healy, Tom Breen, Kay Burke, Maeve Kenny, Evelyn Gordon and Marie-Thérèse Devins.

Finally, the authors are indebted to Michael Littleton, Paddy Glackin and Michael Croke, all of Radio Telefís Éireann, who together with Mary Feehan and John Spillane, of Mercier Press, have supported this project from the beginning.

GROWING UP

BETWEEN THE AGES OF 11–18, adolescents experience the most dramatic transformation in their physical, emotional, and psychological development. The changes that take place, from adolescence to adulthood, are of a magnitude not seen since the first six years of the boy's or girl's life.

This is a time of great energy, creativity, vulnerability, sensitivity and turmoil. It is a time when adolescents evaluate themselves in the context of their peers, as they struggle from childhood to become a man or a woman.

It is also a time when the core values of self-esteem and self-worth come into their own, determining just how well adolescents cope with the pressures they face and how well they develop and prepare themselves for the challenges in their lives ahead.

For parents, the challenge lies in striking a delicate balance between, on the one hand, establishing rules of behaviour and fostering the growth of the child, while, on the other hand, allowing the child sufficient independence and freedom to strike out on his or her own.

It must be remembered that this is the stage when adolescents have begun 'leaving home'; a time when they are severing the bonds with their family and establishing an individual identity that will prepare them for survival during the rest of their lives.

How they cope will depend on many factors, including the following:

- Biological make-up, genetic endowment, and gender.
- Personality and temperamental disposition, their capacity to relate to others, and the response of others to them.

- Social and cultural factors, including prevailing views about adolescence and young people in general, media messages, and marketing strategies geared towards adolescents.
- Family size: whether first born, second born, youngest, or other position within the family.
- The ease or difficulty of birth and labour, whether birth followed closely on the birth of a brother or sister, and whether the child was welcome and wanted.
- The mother's post-natal status (general health, depression, fatigue), and general family dynamics at the time the adolescent was born.
- Family history, including trans-generational history, heredity, family myths and stories, family beliefs and fears.
- The status of parents: whether famous, infamous, depressed, alcoholic, able, disadvantaged, gifted, creative, or talented.
- Marital status of parents: whether widowed, single, divorced, or remarried.
- Relationship with parents, and the degree to which the relationship is positive with both of the parents.
- Relationship with brothers and sisters, half-brothers and half-sisters, or stepbrothers and stepsisters.
- Environment at home, coping capacity of parents, and practical parenting styles.
- Supports available from the extended family, including grandparents, aunts, uncles, and cousins. Also, proximity of extended family to the adolescent, both geographically and emotionally.
- Relationship and connection with other boys and girls, and support available from this source.
- Location of family home, and its connection or isolation from the community in general and from adolescent peers in particular.

- Life events, including specific stressors such as accidents or trauma.
- Medical history, including experience of prolonged illness, time spent in hospital, and time lost from school.
- Intellectual ability, academic achievement, and belief in intellectual and vocational possibilities.
- Level of confidence and self-esteem built up during the childhood years.

All of these factors come together to shape the child arriving at adolescence. By this stage, many markers have already been laid down for the years ahead. Strengths and vulnerabilities have been identified, and life experiences may have already tested the resources and resilience of the young person. Indeed, the childhood pattern of emotional experience is one of the best predictors of either a stormy or a stress-free adolescence. An uneventful childhood is invariably followed by an uneventful adolescence.

What lies ahead need not be feared. The notion of adolescence exclusively as a time of 'storm and stress' has been replaced by a new understanding of the positive relationships and experiences that adolescents and their parents can share during this challenging 'second edition of childhood'. At this stage, the adolescent's challenges and tasks include the following:

- Abandoning childhood and embracing adulthood.
- Adapting to a new and ever-changing body.
- Renegotiating the relationship with parents from dependence to independence.
- Establishing friendships, acquiring social skills, and learning how to handle opposite-sex relationships.
- Resisting peer pressure, especially regarding the taking of alcohol and drugs, or engaging in sexual activity or delinquent acts.

- Dealing with emotions ranging from delight to despair, elation to apathy, self-esteem to self-deprecation, confidence to confusion, and hope to hopelessness.
- Coping with the transition from Junior School to Secondary School, and sitting examinations such as the Junior Certificate, Leaving Certificate, and Third Level examinations.
- Deciding on future career choices.
- Establishing a personal identity, a 'sense of self', a good body-image, and personal and social confidence.

PHYSICAL CHANGES

To understand the process of adolescent growth and development, we need first to understand the enormous physical changes being experienced at this stage in life. Any parent attending a first year, Secondary School function will be struck by the range of shapes, heights and body sizes: fat, thin, long, short, long-limbed, awkward, in proportion, disproportionate, or trapped physiologically between childhood and adulthood. The process we are talking about is 'puberty', which is the period of most rapid change, accelerated growth and sexual maturation. During this stage, the adolescent undergoes the following changes:

- Changes in height and weight.
- A redistribution of body fat.
- Changes in the rate of metabolism.
- Secretion of a range of hormones.
- Development of sexual characteristics, such as the appearance of breasts.
- Changes in the larynx, affecting the voice.
- Growth of body hair.
- Change in body shape and proportions.
- Sexual 'stirrings', and physical arousal.

Adolescents have the task of emerging from puberty and acquiring an adult identity. This involves relinquishing the physique and the accompanying physical and psychological identity of childhood, and adjusting to a new identity as young men and young women. How well this process is managed is crucial in determining the adolescent's future respect for their body, their attitude to healthy eating, care about what is ingested into the body (such as drugs, alcohol, cigarettes), and their development of a healthy self-concept and body image.

EMOTIONAL DEVELOPMENT

Many parents dread the teenage years because of the overwhelming range of moods and emotions which adolescents experience. During adolescence, emotions may be exceptionally varied, extreme and conflicting. It is a time when life is experienced in a vivid and intense manner. There is an intensity of emotional attachments to friends, to boyfriends, or to girlfriends.

Furthermore, adolescents often react in an extreme manner: with anger, temper, grief and mourning; with joy and exuberance; with profound sadness and empathy; with gross insensitivity, ridicule and derision; with an acute sense of injustice (particularly if unfairly criticised by a parent or teacher); with idealism and an ethical passion about various 'rights' and 'causes'.

There are also many worries in teenagers' lives. High on the list are worries about school, home, relationships with parents, relationships with peers, and vocational choices for the future. The following are some examples:

- Fear of academic failure, worry about relationships with teachers, doubts about ability in classroom subjects, and uncertainty about capacity to complete homework and

11

study tasks.

- Worry about examinations. As many as 66% of Irish Secondary School students express this as a primary worry in their lives.

- Concern about family, particularly the health and well-being of family members. Fears may be voiced about a parent becoming seriously ill, a father dying of a heart attack, or a mother having cancer. It is estimated that these factors generate worry for over one-half of adolescents.

- Upset about the inevitable conflict with parents, as adolescents struggle with the joy of independence and the loss of the special childhood closeness to parents.

- Worries about shyness, about the capacity to communicate effectively, the need to integrate with the peer group, to be liked by others, to be popular, and to be invited to parties and other activities.

- Worry about the lack of certainty in life. The loss of a secure, unreflective 'self', and adjustment to a new, volatile and ever-changing 'self'.

- Preoccupation with physical appearance. Worry about acne, weight, physique, height, and general good looks.

- Worries about psychological disposition; about being 'normal'; about being suspicious, jealous, troubled, obsessive, panicky, compulsive, anxious, depressed; about ability to cope with reality, with change, with relationships, and with life.

SEXUAL CHANGES

During adolescence, self-consciousness and self-awareness are brought to a head by the onslaught of the dramatic physical changes that take place. Adolescents seek to understand their bodies, to learn about menstruation, nocturnal emission, involuntary erections, masturbation (90% of boys and 70% of girls masturbate). Adolescents must also come to terms with sexual fantasies, sexual activity, contraception and pregnancy, and must find ways to establish responsible and loving relationships. They also have to reconcile this process of self-evaluation with the values and the models of behaviour of their parents, which can be particularly strong and influential in determining adolescent sexual behaviour.

Adolescents have to establish a code of sexual behaviour that is a subtle blend of peer views, media constructions, societal mores, religious beliefs and parental attitudes, while also incorporating their gender role, their values, and personal awareness of their own bodies. This is a difficult process, requiring adolescents to achieve the following:

- Acquire information on reproduction and on sexuality. Studies show that 62% of Irish adolescents say that they talk to their mothers about sex, and 16% talk to their fathers. Approximately 5% of adolescents acquire information from their teachers.
- Seek information on sex from other sources, such as friends, siblings, the media, and by reading books and magazines.
- Understand sexuality in the context of relationships. Many adolescents are well-educated on anatomical facts, but express less certainty about relationships.
- Balance biological urges with confused, contradictory and uncertain messages. This involves reconciling liberating and joyous concepts of sex (loving relationships, motherhood, caring and sharing) with images of sex as cruel and coercive (sexual abuse, rape, pornography).

INTELLECTUAL CHANGES
Intellectual ability, while having some stability over time, is not as fixed as many people imagine. It can be enriched, expanded,

13

broadened, refined, directed, and brought to full potential, or neglected, dampened, depressed, and used to minimal effect. Knowledge and mental skills develop rapidly from the time we are born until we arrive at adolescence. During adolescence, a number of particular skills appear for the first time, including the capacity to achieve the following:

- To test against the facts.
- To shift from concrete to abstract thinking.
- To imagine the possible, and to hypothesise.
- To deduce information by analysis or argument.
- To consider varying views and opinions, and to analyse their validity.
- To construct propositions, and to make connections between them.
- To understand the concept of a theoretical position.

The teenage years are a period of considerable intellectual activity, and many imperceptible changes take place in the adolescent's intellectual capacity. These include the ability to understand, to form concepts, to reason, to develop abstract ideas, to develop an overview of a problem, to appreciate the opinions and writings of others, to calculate, to absorb abstract mathematical concepts, and to enjoy the beauty or aesthetics of an arrangement of words in poetry, novels or prose.

Unfortunately, serious intellectual or academic problems may cause the adolescent to become deeply unhappy, to withdraw, to refuse to attend school, or to become aggressive, disruptive and even delinquent.

Developmental disorders, language disorders and written language disorders, problems with speech, pronunciation, language and communicative ability, along with specific reading, spelling and writing problems are more common amongst boys

14

than girls (by a ratio of 4–1). The adolescent's happiness in school, sense of achievement, ability to display knowledge in examinations, and general ease in the world are obviously affected by such conditions.

Add to this the pressure of examinations, a points system that determines access to, or denial of, vocational choice, and a culture that tends to reward academic success above other talents and skills, and one can understand the degree to which intellectual capacity affects the adolescent's self-esteem at the deepest level.

PERSONALITY CHANGES

Establishing a personal identity is the central task of adolescence. The question 'Who am I?' is pivotal to the adolescent in developing a 'sense of self'. The answer is acquired through the responses of parents, friends, teachers, the media, and even by scrutinising the reflection in the mirror.

Frequently, adolescents are confused about their identity, and have a much clearer understanding of who they are *not*. This is why they so frequently use phrases with their parents such as 'I am not a child' or 'I am not like you'.

In effect, the adolescent is seeking to be an individual, to have a separate, recognisable and distinct identity. Therefore, much of the conflict that takes place between adolescents and parents, while ostensibly being disagreements about practical things (such as body adornment, clothes, hairstyles, choice of music), are really about the adolescent asserting the right to be an individual.

Identity is a pivotal issue at any stage of life, but is particularly so during adolescence when the old identity of childhood has to be replaced. The adolescent no longer has the identity of a child, but is not yet ready to claim the identity of an adult. In the process of moving from one stage to the next, adolescents are likely to attempt the following:

- Experiment with different styles of appearance, including clothes.
- Try out different 'roles' and styles of behaviour.
- Test different techniques of social interaction and social discourse.
- Experiment with different social responses, such as aggression or compliance.
- Try out different personality styles 'for size'.
- Test boundaries, to see how far they can be stretched.
- Establish their social status, their 'standing', and their position of power.
- Provoke others, to test their responses and reactions.

PROBLEMS THAT MIGHT ARISE

Substantial distress can occur for many teenagers during the adolescent years. Studies suggest that more than one in five young people will, at some stage and for short periods, experience feelings of misery, excessive sensitivity, low self-worth and low self-esteem.

There is also evidence that four out of ten adolescents will feel miserable or depressed. One in five have problems sleeping, and one in twelve will think about suicide.

Despite the fact that many adults reject the notion of adolescents being depressed, the process of growing up can lead teenagers to become 'fed-up', 'down' or 'distressed' to such an extent that they might consider taking their own lives. There are many sources of stress during the teenage years which may cause adolescents to feel this way. They include the following:

- Shyness, and experiencing difficulties establishing friendships.

16

- Being the victim of bullying.
- Experiencing confusion concerning sexuality and in relations with the opposite sex.
- Encountering problems at school, and experiencing examination pressure.
- Being exposed to alcohol and drugs, and developing addictions.
- Being victimised by excessive discipline, or by sexual and physical abuse.
- Encountering family problems, as a result of separation or divorce.
- Developing serious eating disorders.
- Developing behavioural problems, including delinquency.
- Experiencing grief, shock and anxiety following a first bereavement.

THE ROLE OF THE PARENT

During adolescence, the parent moves from the protective nurturer of the child and becomes a facilitator who guides and directs the young person to the calmer world of adulthood. It is only when adolescents can survive without their parents that the parents' task is successfully completed.

The role of parents in helping their child through the teenage years cannot be overestimated. Parents are central to the development of the health, happiness, esteem, and intellectual capacity of the adolescent. They act as behavioural models for their children, and provide a source of security, strength and love in the adolescent's life. Therefore, parents need to achieve the following:

- Foster self-esteem.
- Provide a safe environment.
- Encourage friendships.

- Provide positive support at all times.
- Desist from negative criticism.
- Retain a belief in the goodness, the value and the integrity of the adolescent.
- Show respect for the adolescent's ideas and opinions.
- Provide love, care and affection.
- Offer support with studies, and recognise the adolescent's talents.
- Provide constant recognition of their worth, and stress the contribution they have to make.
- Never abandon them, but gradually let them go.

In time, adolescents grow up, and the battles, struggles, worries and fears settle down into a period of quiescence and stability, predictability and certainty.

As parents look back on the few short years of adolescence, they often wonder what the fear and drama was about. They remind themselves that living with teenagers was not a terminal illness, that adolescence was not a disease, and that time quickly resolved the problems.

That, however, is when the process is over and done. For us, in this book, the problems, the traumas, the intensity and the conflicts of adolescence are only about to begin.

SEXUALITY

OUR SEX ASSIGNED AT BIRTH is a significant factor in determining how we understand ourselves and live out our lives. In childhood, gender is simply a matter of knowing that one is a 'girl' or a 'boy' and accepting the dress and behaviours that are assigned to these roles. In adolescence, the young person faces the task of consciously assimilating the prescribed gender and sexual roles, thereby moving from the innocence of childhood to adult physiological and psychological sexual maturity. It is not surprising that young people suffer enormous stress and confusion in the process.

Adolescence is a time of dramatic physiological change, beginning with puberty. It involves the struggle with sexual awakenings and with feelings that may even be frightening. It includes the pain of learning about relationships and about how to form rewarding opposite-sex attachments.

Additionally, the young adolescent faces a proliferation of mixed and sometimes contradictory societal messages about sexuality. Therefore, it is not surprising that the issue of sexuality is a confused one for young people. For many adolescents the normal confusions are exacerbated by the following:

- Media-generated portrayals of sexuality, which define women as 'objects' and which depict men primarily in 'macho' or 'coercive' roles.
- Advertising, which sells commodities by associating them with sexual images of men or (more often) of women.
- Portrayals that rate men on 'performance' and rate women on 'submission'.
- Pornographic images that equate sex with violence, cruelty, sadism and power. Depictions of women as sexual com-

modities, and depictions of men as commodity users.

- Societal double standards that allow men to be 'admired' for sexual activity, while women are 'sanctioned' for sexual behaviour.
- Differing terminology used to describe female sexuality and male sexuality. One study found that there are 220 negative words for female sexual activity (e.g., 'slut') and only 20 mainly positive words (e.g., 'stud') to define male sexuality.
- The message to boys that male urges are uncontrollable, while the strong message to girls is that they are responsible for male sexual urges and their control. There are no clear message to boys and girls that each person is responsible for their *own* sexuality and behaviour.

TEENAGE CONFUSION ABOUT SEXUALITY

Looked at from the young teenager's perspective, there are enormous difficulties procuring accurate and comprehensive information regarding the physiological and emotional process of sexual development. Because of embarrassment and ignorance, together with societal ambivalence and discomfort, it is difficult for teenagers to understand and to come to terms with what is going on.

As a result of this lack of information, misinformation, negative information and conflicting messages, it is hardly surprising that boys and girls struggle in their behaviour towards each other. Therefore, they may experience the following:

- Wishing they were still children, while simultaneously wishing they were grown up. Being uncertain about what they want to be and losing a sense of identity, can often result during the passage from childhood to adolescence.
- Experiencing discomfort with the turbulent and erratic

physiological changes of puberty. Being embarrassed, excited, ashamed, and delighted by such changes.

- Switching from the childhood stance of essentially 'ignoring' the opposite sex to a stance where both sexes engage in friendships with each other.
- Not knowing how to talk to a member of the opposite sex, and wondering whether the correct way to do so should be based on media models, in the manner prescribed by parents, or in the manner prescribed by peers.
- Wondering what the opposite sex really looks like. Being fearful and excited about the prospect of finding out.
- Maturing earlier or later than peers, and being uncomfortable as a result of comparisons.
- Being embarrassed in sports changing-rooms, especially when dressing or undressing.
- Experiencing worries or shame about masturbation, and believing it to be responsible for conditions ranging from acne to infertility.
- Having fantasies about sex, and experiencing discomfort about those fantasies.
- Finding it difficult to deal with sexualised comments about appearance. Girls and boys find that their changed bodies can be sources of sexual innuendo in conversation, both with each other and with the wider adult world.
- Being unable to discuss sex with parents, or finding that parents avoid, show embarrassment and inhibition, or provide minimal information that is more cautionary ('Don't do it') than helpful.
- Being worried about the sexual expectations of others, particularly messages that rank sexual 'performance' or 'prowess' as primary.
- Worrying about homosexuality, and wondering if the closeness of same-sex friendships means that you are 'gay'.

- 'Falling in love', and being overwhelmed by the intensity of first love.
- Being rejected by a girlfriend or boyfriend, and being overwhelmed by the intensity and agony of the loss.
- Being rejected at discos, and therefore feeling isolated and unattractive. Alternatively, discovering that you are popular at social events and wondering how to deal with such newly-discovered 'power'.
- Worrying about how to ask for a date from a member of the opposite sex, and worrying about the crushing fear of rejection if the request is refused.
- Finding that adults treat adolescent attachments with amusement, derision, disregard, or lack of understanding. Using phrases such as, 'There are more fish in the sea' is unhelpful.
- Becoming aware that one's parents are sexual beings. In instances of separation or divorce, having to cope with the sexual implications of a parent taking on a new partner can be distressing.
- In some situations of sexual abuse, finding that one becomes an object of sexual interest to parents, step-parents or other adults in whom trust has been placed.
- For boys, being treated suspiciously as a result of their physical development. For example, it is often alarming for boys walking home at night to discover that they are treated as a source of threat or danger by women they encounter on the street.
- For girls, becoming aware of the threat from the opposite sex. For example, it is often alarming for young girls to realise that they are the potential victims of attack. It is estimated that 50% of rape victims come from the adolescent population.

PHYSIOLOGICAL CHANGES

The beginning of sexual maturation is accompanied by the 'growth spurt', which refers to the key period of accelerated increase in height and weight. Puberty refers to the stage when the visible signs of physical sexual maturity appear. In girls, puberty is marked by the onset of menstruation (periods). It is less easy to define in boys, but involves the growth in physical or secondary sexual characteristics.

Girls tend to enter the 'growth spurt' and puberty earlier than boys. Generally, girls begin puberty at approximately 10–11 years, and boys enter roughly two years later, at approximately 12–13 years, although there is great variability in this process. By 16 years, most girls will have achieved sexual maturity. Most boys will have done so by 18 years of age.

Studies show that the age at which one enters the 'growth spurt' can have psychological effects on the young person, particularly if it is earlier or later than peers. Some studies show that early-maturing boys are often psychologically better adjusted than late-maturing boys, being taller, larger, stronger, and rated as more attractive than their late-maturing peers, who may feel 'feminine' and 'weedy'.

Conversely, early-maturing girls can feel 'massive' or 'huge', as they tower above their peers. They may look more sexually developed, and are therefore at risk of sexual comment or even sexual advances that the child within them is unable to handle. Also, because girls tend to enter puberty earlier than boys, the development of early-maturing girls may be grossly at variance with that of late-maturing boys. This is an uncomfortable situation for both boys and girls.

Although this section focuses on physiological changes at puberty, it is important not to describe adolescence, or even puberty, in purely biological terms. The changes in adolescence are the result of many factors which are interrelated, including the following:

- *Social factors*, which include the views, beliefs, attitudes and behaviours of a society, at any one point in time.
- *Cognitive (intellectual) abilities*, which include the intellectual capacity of the young person to understand and make sense of their personal life, and to understand the world in general.
- *Emotional capacities and responses*, including prior emotional experiences and current emotional feelings. These also include the emotional responses of others to the adolescent and how they feel about such responses.
- *Biological factors*, including all the hormonal, physical and bodily experiences, and their effect on mood.

It is how these interact or influence each other that is the determining factor in how adolescents negotiate their way through this stage of life. This interaction also determines how they come to understand their sexuality and live out their lives as sexual beings, not only in adolescence but into adulthood and beyond.

BOYS AND GIRLS WORRIES ABOUT PHYSICAL DEVELOPMENT

Both boys and girls worry about the purely physical aspects of puberty. There are chemical changes to get used to, 'growth spurts' to accommodate, new moods to cope with, appearance changes to come to terms with, and ever-evolving transformations in bodily size and bodily functions that need to be adapted to. The resulting confusion can generate many concerns for adolescents:

Boys
- Feeling a lack of control over the body, particularly over erections.

- Being surprised or embarrassed by nocturnal emissions (wet dreams).
- Comparing penis size with peers, and worrying that there is a great difference. Believing that this is a reflection of masculinity.
- Having an excessively hairy chest or no chest hairs at all. It is not unknown for boys to count the chest hairs and to carefully guard the few that appear.
- Searching for facial hair, and fearing that it will never grow. Being inexperienced at shaving, and finding it uncomfortable, especially if the face and neck are 'spotty'.
- Having increased breast growth during puberty, which may be alarming for boys if it happens. However, when hormones settle this should disappear.
- Experiencing voice changes. As the larynx grows, the voice becomes deeper. This growth is greater in boys than girls, and it is this growth which forms the 'Adam's apple'.
- Being worried about what their body might look like to a girl.

Girls
- Having to cope with cramps, pains, headaches and backache during periods. Being uncomfortable about partaking in sports, particularly swimming.
- Feeling 'fed up', depressed, 'touchy' and tense as a result of premenstrual tension.
- Worrying about the difference in breast size compared to peers. Feeling uncomfortable if breasts are particularly well developed. Feeling 'childish' if development is slight.
- Worrying if one breast develops more than the other, and not knowing that this can be normal.
- Being concerned about the correct sanitary protection to use, such as tampons or pads, and not having anyone to ask

for advice. Also, worrying about cautions on the packets concerning 'toxic shock'.

- Being worried about what their body might look like to a boy.

GIRLS AND BOYS WORRIES ABOUT EMOTIONAL DEVELOPMENT
While many of the emotional reactions of young people to sexuality are similar, there are differences between boys and girls both in general emotional expression and in the emotions surrounding their sexuality. Many of these emotional responses are determined in childhood, when girls tend to be rewarded for compliant, sensitive and non-aggressive behaviour, while boys receive encouragement and less punishment for aggressive behaviour.

Parents are more likely to encourage a boy to 'fight his corner', whereas girls are more likely to be reprimanded. Girls are allowed to cry, and are consoled when they do so. Boys are often discouraged from any 'feminine' behaviours or overly emotional displays. This is epitomised by the expression, 'Big boys don't cry'.

It is not surprising, therefore, that the emotional responses of boys and girls to adolescent sexuality may differ. The following are of note:

- Boys have been found to be more pragmatic and less emotional about sexual activity, and general sexual activity has been found to be higher in boys.
- Girls tend to be motivated more by the idealised or romantic aspects of relationships. Boys tend to be motivated more by sexual gratification.
- Boys tend to show less need for emotional attachment as a prerequisite for engaging in sexual activity. Girls tend to prioritise 'love' as the reason for engaging in sexual activity.

- Girls' relationships tend to be subject more to jealousy than boys relationships. Boys tend to be more competitive and concerned with sexual status and prowess.

WHAT CAN PARENTS DO?

There is a lack of adult consensus, and a not inconsiderable public debate, on the appropriate sexual education and behaviour for young people. Parents need to position themselves from the standpoint of their own ethical beliefs, all the time ensuring that clear, compassionate and helpful information is provided to adolescents. This is necessary to counteract any confusion and to help adolescents who are trying to understand sexuality in general and their own sexuality in particular.

Parents can help young people to be comfortable with, and responsible for, their growing concern about sexuality in the following ways:

- Ensure that your sons and daughters have the required information to prepare them for puberty. Remember that what you tell them will shape their expectations and attitudes as they grow up.
- Take responsibility for the sexual education of adolescents. Many parents are caught, on the one hand, between concerns about what their children will learn if sex education is provided elsewhere and, on the other hand, their anxiety or difficulty in providing sex education themselves.
- Talk to your adolescent about sexuality and reproduction in a realistic, informed, relaxed and caring manner.
- The facts about reproduction should be expressed in a simple, straightforward fashion, avoiding confusing references where possible (e.g., 'birds and bees', 'storks', etc.).
- Explain the reproductive process in the context of normal emotions and the normal 'hugs' and physical contacts that

27

take place between the sexes.

- Advise the adolescent about the dangers of sexual diseases, such as venereal disease, and emphasise the dangers of AIDS being transmitted.
- Explain what is happening when 'wet dreams' occur, and describe the menstrual process to your daughter well in advance.
- It is probably better not to discuss masturbation, and allow such activities to the privacy of the teenager.
- Help young people to respect themselves, and teach respect, not shame, about their bodies.
- Encourage adolescents to reject sexual stereotyping, and to regard themselves as individuals first and gendered individuals second.
- Actively discourage the use of sexually denigrating language by teenagers. It can take years for a young girl to recover from being called a 'slut' or a 'tart'.
- Explain to sons and daughters about rape, including the following: that most rapists are known to their victims, that women do not ask to be raped, that most rapes are planned, that rape is about power and humiliation and hatred, not about sex, and that rapists come from all classes in society.
- Teach sons and daughters that sex is not compulsory, that saying *no* is fine, and that the choice is always theirs.
- Do not explain adolescent sexual behaviour exclusively in terms of consequences, such as pregnancy. Reaching sexual maturity has many more dimensions than simply avoiding pregnancy.
- Teach young people that sexual freedoms and sexual rights carry sexual obligations and sexual responsibilities.
- Continue to be affectionate, caring and concerned about your teenagers, so that they do not misguidedly seek 'affect-

ion' in sexual activity with peers. Sexual activity should not be a replacement for parental affection.

- Do not mock the adolescent's attachments, crushes and loves. Phrases such as, 'It's only puppy love' are deeply insulting to the young person.
- Explain to the adolescent the needs and requirements for increased hygiene during adolescence, e.g., skin or vaginal hygiene.
- Advise an adolescent about the range of medications and treatments for acne, and seek professional help if necessary.
- Respect a teenager's privacy, in particular the privacy of their bedrooms, the privacy of their thoughts, and the privacy of their fantasies.
- Monitor television, film and video viewing, particularly any pornographic video material that might be present in the home.
- Permit friendships with both sexes as early as possible during early adolescence. This allows girls and boys the time to get to know each other as people and as friends.
- Welcome their friends, girlfriends and boyfriends, and be pleased that they have established friendships.
- Help them to understand that a mature relationship, based on understanding and equality between people, is important.
- Parents should examine their own double standards regarding sexuality. Additionally, they should have equal concern about the sexual values of their sons and daughters.
- Parents need to provide clear boundaries about sexual behaviour. As with any adolescent behaviour, limits and boundaries are a sign of parental concern and care, and young people are more comfortable when these boundaries are clear.
- Allow them to enjoy being young, exuberant, in love, happy,

and encourage them to enjoy this stage of their life.

How an adolescent copes with the sexual problems of the teen-age years depends on the messages that we provide to teen-agers about themselves, their bodies, their value, their worth, their behaviour. While public beliefs shift and change, adoles-cents remain essentially the same from one generation to the next, and differences in behaviour depend on how they are edu-cated, what they are taught, and the relationship we have with them when we try to guide them.

Parents need not be overly worried about their teenager's sexual behaviour. By taking an active role in providing inform-ation, setting standards, establishing rules, offering advice and providing emotional support and encouragement, parents have considerable power to shape that behaviour. How success-ful they are will depend on the relationship with their teenager and the model of beliefs and behaviour they themselves present.

FRIENDS

A LIFE WITHOUT FRIENDS WOULD be desolate and barren. Friends provide many important supports; acting as partners with whom we can share enjoyable activities, companions with whom we can safely share our worries, persons to rescue us if we are in difficulty, or confidantes to comfort us at times of stress or loss.

During childhood, we find our friends primarily at school, through meeting children of our parents' friends, from neighbouring houses or nearby estates, playing with brothers or sisters, or by meeting other children while attending activities such as dancing class, karate, scouts, local tennis clubs, and other extracurricular activities.

During adolescence, the network of friendships widens, and teenagers may have many acquaintances who are not necessarily known to their parents. Young people spend increasing time with companions, and there is a strong need to fit into and belong to a network of friends.

Additionally, adolescents begin to form opposite-sex friendships and to move about in groups consisting of both boys and girls. This can be exciting and challenging, or it can cause stress and embarrassment.

Forming good and positive friendships is an integral part of the young person's social and psychological development. These friendships can be an important supplement to parental support through the teenage years, by achieving the following:

- Allowing the move towards independence, which is part of the adolescent process of separation from parents.
- Providing help with the socialising process. This help may be necessary in today's world because of declining family

size and curtailments in the extended family.

- Learning about group conformity, and considering peer values as well as parental values.
- Introducing young people to members of the opposite sex. This is an important preparation for heterosexual relationships and for learning how to form these relationships in future years.
- Providing a connection with others who are at the same stage of development and who share similar upsets, stresses and difficulties.
- Providing understanding and support to adolescents, particularly at a time of life when they do not perceive these comforts as coming from parents.
- Counterbalancing existing negative experiences or views of males and females. For example, an adolescent girl with a strict or rejecting father may learn that other males can be warm and nurturing. Alternatively, a boy with a mother who is demanding or critical may experience other females as accepting and supportive.
- Protecting the teenager from loneliness or isolation in the many tasks of growing up.
- Testing a teenager's competence in relation to others of similar age, which may not be possible in families where brothers and sisters are younger or older.
- Enabling the adolescent to be part of a 'clique' or part of a 'crowd', and providing the teenager with a 'sense of belonging'.
- Allowing the teenager to establish 'best friends'. Best friends provide understanding, partnership, companionship, and act as a source of solace for the adolescent.
- Providing peer reassurance, encouragement, or help with study and examinations.
- Developing an age-appropriate sense of humour. Finding

out what works, or does not work, in communication is important for later life interaction.

- Learning how to accommodate the wishes of others, and how to assert one's own wishes through negotiation.
- Trying out various identities or roles, by participating in different friendship groups or situations.
- Discovering that other friends' families live differently, thereby helping to challenge prejudices and to develop tolerances.
- Having others around who share the adolescent's idealism, spiritual values and their concept of adult fallibility.
- Accepting advice and constructive criticism that would not be tolerated from parents.

PEER VERSUS PARENTAL INFLUENCES

While parents are anxious that their children have friends that belong to their own age group, many parents are also concerned that the peer group will begin to exercise negative influence and excessive control.

Studies suggest that parents who have a 'warm' relationship with their teenager have little to fear in this respect. In fact, many research studies show that the conflict between parent and peer influence is not as great as many parents believe, provided that parents are in a good relationship with their adolescent.

Because friends are often drawn from the same social, economic and educational groupings as the teenager, there is often compatibility between the general aspirations of parents and peer groups. Furthermore, studies show that parental influence still predominates when it comes to fundamental issues such as social and moral values, whereas peer values predominate with regard to style of dress, hairstyles, and choice of music.

In one Irish survey, 98% of young teenagers (12–15 years) rated parents' behaviour as having the greatest influence and relevance to how they would live their lives. In this study, while friends were important to 97% of the teenagers, they were *not* more influential than parents. Additionally, as many as 97% of these teenagers also rated their families as 'really important' to them.

Studies of adolescents suggest that peer influences become dominant when the young person perceives a lack of concern or affection at home. Additionally, adolescents are most at risk in *early* adolescence, because this is the time of greatest conformity and the time when the young person is most likely to succumb to negative behaviour.

Clinical findings also show that when parents do not know where their adolescents are, who they are with, or when they will return home, the opportunities for dangerous peer activities increase. Additionally, when uncontrolled adolescents are upset and distressed, they are more likely to turn to risk-taking or substance abuse, instead of seeking emotional help from their parents.

Furthermore, in situations of marital conflict, separation and divorce, adolescents can feel betrayed, lose trust in adults, and turn to the peer group for support. However, much will depend on the psychological strength and skill of separated or divorced parents in coping with the situation.

Young people who are unhappy at home are also more likely to form alliances with those who are equally disenchanted and with those over whom little parental control is exercised. This may lead them to join a peer group consisting of disturbed adolescents.

Finally, clinical findings support the importance and influence that parents have in their adolescents' lives, and suggest that it is primarily when the parent/teenager relationship breaks down, that adolescents become particularly susceptible to negative peer influences.

NEGATIVE PEER INFLUENCES
There are many instances where peer influence may become negative and disruptive, leading the young person into difficult and even dangerous situations. The following are some of the potential negative peer behaviours and interactions to which an adolescent may be vulnerable:

- Encouraging the young person to challenge parental views and to dismiss them without due consideration.
- Introducing the adolescent to alcohol, cigarettes, or illegal drugs.
- Persuading the adolescent to join in risk-taking activities, such as shoplifting, joyriding, or other delinquent acts.
- Inflicting cruel, bullying or neglectful behaviour on the adolescent, thereby diminishing self-esteem.
- Encouraging the adolescent to join in gangs, with the intention of bullying others.
- Requiring the adolescent to conform excessively to the peer group, slavishly follow fashions, or engage in practices such as excessive body-piercing with the attendant risks of infection or scarring of the body.
- Inviting, or coercing, the young person into premature sexual activity, and ridiculing or denigrating those who do not participate.
- Persuading the young person to abandon educational aspirations, or mocking the teenager who achieves good results.
- Enticing the teenager to spend minimal time with the family, thereby leading the adolescent into family conflict.
- Encouraging school truancy, or behaviour at school that is

likely to result in serious discipline or suspension.

- Introducing the teenager to sexualised and offensive language, which may then be used with parents or brothers and sisters.
- Encouraging the adolescent to participate in aggressive or hostile behaviour towards others, such as elderly people, or those with a handicap or a physical deformity.
- Provoking the adolescent to participate in acts of vandalism or criminal activity.

DIFFERENCES BETWEEN GIRLS AND BOYS IN MAKING FRIENDS

In general, studies have found that male identity is threatened by intimacy, and female identity is threatened by separation. This makes the task of understanding each other more difficult for adolescents. Additionally, boys and girls exhibit some different behaviours with regard to same-sex and opposite-sex friendships, including the following:

- When interacting with others, girls are more likely to express their emotions than boys.
- Boys favour same-sex groups and gangs, whereas girls tend to have individual same-sex friendships, particularly in early adolescence. However, cliques of special friends are also important to girls at that stage.
- Girls tend to disclose greater amounts of personal information to each other than boys.
- Boys' interactions tend to be more activity oriented, whereas girls generally meet for conversation or for the exchange of confidences.

YOUNG PEOPLE WHO CAN'T MAKE FRIENDS

Some young people bask in the glow of seemingly permanent popularity. They are temperamentally more outgoing, communicative and friendly, and have a wide range of friends. Other adolescents (particularly girls) are content to have at least one or two good friends, affording them access to wider groups.

Many adolescents experience periods of isolation, particularly in instances where a family moves home or an adolescent changes school. In such cases, it is difficult to enter into a group where members know each other well, and it can take time to learn the rules and interests of group members and to be accepted by them.

The transition from Junior to Secondary School can be particularly overwhelming. This transition requires academic and social adjustments that often coincide with the already daunting adaptations to puberty. Additionally, many Secondary Schools have several first year classes, amounting to an overwhelming number of peers which the new arrival has to get to know. Of course, it is easier if some Junior School friends also transfer to the same Secondary School, thereby establishing a clique which the adolescent may gravitate towards in his new academic surroundings.

Intellectual and learning difficulties (especially language and written language disorders) often emerge for the first time in Secondary School. Homework is likely to be more complicated, and parents are likely to be less involved or less able to help their children with their academic exercises.

The upset of being unable to cope academically can be distressing to the young person, especially if a parent's expectations are not in tune with the adolescent's true ability. This can cause some teenagers to hide their intellectual and academic difficulties in disruptive class behaviour or to form alliances with other disruptive and non-compliant peers. Alternatively, they may withdraw from others because of embarrassment, or they may be rejected by their peers.

It is estimated that as many as 20% of young people, in any

school year, may find themselves being shunned or isolated. Social rejection is an acute and painful experience for the young person, attacking the core of their emotional happiness and self-esteem. The following factors may be associated with such rejection:

- Being different, being unattractive physically, or being over-weight. Early adolescence is a time of peak group conformity. Radical differences tend to make the group anxious and intolerant.
- Being excessively shy. The behaviours of those who are excessively shy or socially phobic tend to be off-putting. Shy adolescents will frequently make poor eye contact, hide their faces, and become so preoccupied with their embarrassment that they come across as 'cold', 'aloof', or 'odd'.
- Having communicative disorders. Adolescents with these problems may behave oddly, bombard others with facts, and use unusual, quaint or bizarre language. They do not understand the rules of communication, such as taking turns in conversation, sticking to the topic, and showing appropriate emotional responses or reactions.
- Being too narcissistic, self-centred or selfish, or overly demanding of support without reciprocation.
- Being too eager, too 'clingy', overly seeking popularity, or being too emotionally dependent on friendships.
- Not listening to others, or not showing concern for others.
- Growing up in a family that is highly self-sufficient, thereby restricting contact with others. In such a situation, the adolescent may not learn about non-family interactions.
- Being regularly ill. This disrupts school attendance and interactions with friends, and may generate difficulties for reactivating social activities.
- Having parents who are unsociable and hostile, or who do

not encourage the adolescent to make social contacts.

- Having parents who are overly-protective, and who do not allow the adolescent to engage in ordinary interactions with peers.

- Having less skills than others, such as being unable to swim or having poor athletic ability (particularly a problem for boys).

- Having a history of peer problems in childhood. These problems often extend into adolescence and, indeed, are exacerbated by the tasks of the teenage years.

- Being intellectually less able than others, finding it difficult to engage in repartee, or failing to understand the nuances of topics being discussed.

- Having intellectual capacity that is *exceptionally* advanced, having a vocabulary that is inaccessible to peers, unusual interests in which peers cannot participate, and skills so advanced that they cannot compete. However, studies also show that highly intelligent teenagers can be popular, provided they use their intelligence well in social situations.

- Being emotionally distressed. This can lead to rejection, which further increases the emotional distress. The result is that a 'vicious cycle' of depression/rejection may be established.

- Being disloyal, unfaithful, betraying trust or confidences. Adolescents place a high premium on loyalty in friendships, with the result that acts of disloyalty are not easily forgiven.

WHAT CAN PARENTS DO?

Positive friendships are vital in nurturing and supporting teenagers through the process of growing up. These friendships prepare the young person for their many potential roles in life, especially in their personal life and in the world of work.

Parents have a crucial role to play in helping young people

to form appropriate and positive friendships. The following are some ways a parent can help teenagers in this venture:

- If possible, young people should be helped to form friendships long before adolescence begins. This can be achieved by having friends to the house, by celebrating birthdays with a party for friends, or by providing enough toys for them to share with other children.

- Understand that conformity is important, particularly in early adolescence. Allow the young person to conform on *safe* issues, such as clothes, hairstyles and general appearance.

- Allow young adolescents to spend reasonable time on the phone to friends. This is a common activity amongst early adolescents. The young person who cannot ring their friends may not receive phone calls from them.

- Teach your adolescent the importance of cheerfulness, friendliness, and listening to others. They will learn this most by observing you.

- Encourage teenagers to contact a friend who is ill, to express concern, and to show kind and generous behaviour towards others.

- Provide enough money, so that adolescents are not socially embarrassed. This may merely entail sufficient money to buy their own soft drinks or 'chips' when out with friends.

- Do not provide adolescents with more money than their friends receive. This may be embarrassing to their friends, and can also cause young people to try to 'buy' friendships. Also, they may be courted by others for their finances, not their friendliness.

- Be welcoming to friends, and allow them some privacy to chat with each other.

- Teach them skills, such as swimming, tennis, soccer, so that they will be able to join in these activities without embarrassment.

- Encourage them to widen their network of friends by joining group activities, such as karate classes, drama lessons, swimming, or other sports and recreations.
- Don't be fearful of a young adolescent's opposite-sex friendships. They usually occur amongst large groups and are necessary for learning about the opposite-sex. This is helpful in later adolescence when they begin to go out in couples.
- Listen carefully to an adolescent's complex account of their friends, their problems or uncertainties about relationships. You should be pleased that they choose to share these with you, and that they seek your support and advice.
- If you have a car, take turns with other parents in giving lifts to discos or other events. This helps foster friendships, and provides you with an opportunity to meet the parents of your adolescent's friends.
- Don't embarrass an adolescent in front of friends. Wait until they have left before you express any anger or concern you may have.
- Be pleasant to friends who phone, and if the adolescent is not at home take a message. This shows the adolescent that you regard friendships as important.
- Don't issue endless warnings as the young person is leaving the house, especially when they are in the company of friends. The rules and warnings should be clear at all times, not hurried admonitions that will not be attended to anyway.
- Acquaint yourself with the facts before you accuse them or their friends of any wrongdoing. If they have been involved in any untoward adolescent activity, make your concern known. Help them to take responsibility for whatever they have done and to learn from their mistakes.

41

- Show respect for young people, listen to their views and ideas, but don't commandeer the conversation or take over when their friends arrive.
- Spend money, if you can, to help the teenager with personal hygiene, including taking care of greasy hair, buying cleanser and cream for spots, purchasing deodorants, aftershaves and perfumes. Personal hygiene is important and helps self-confidence.
- Try to provide help for acne. Some prescribed antibiotics are very effective in treating the condition. Pharmacists will be aware of the topical (applied to the skin) products used for cleansing and treating spots.
- Don't have rows with your partner when your adolescent's friends are in the house. This is highly embarrassing for teenagers and will make them fearful of inviting friends home.
- Allow 'slumber parties' for young adolescents. However, check out the videos they are watching, as some videos are highly unsuitable for young people.
- If you feel that you cannot allow the young person to attend a peer event to which 'everyone' is supposedly going, suggest that they blame *you* so they can save face.
- Reassure them that your primary concern is their safety. Also, reassure them that you distrust the *situations* that they may be in, not their *motives* or *integrity*.
- Try not to feel rejected by their preference for time spent with friends rather than with family. You are still essential in their lives, and always will be.

Having friends is crucially important during the adolescent years. Friendships provide a form of support that cannot be acquired elsewhere. Encouraging teenagers to make and retain friends is an important part of parenting, and young people who are isolated and rejected by friends suffer enormously. The importance of guiding young people, from an early age, in forming friendships, developing social confidence, and learning effective interpersonal skills and responses should not be underestimated.

BULLYING

BULLYING IS A SERIOUS, UNACCEPTABLE and incapacitating experience for young people. It interrupts the normal adolescent process and is an experience that may linger and influence many later relationships, if both perpetrator and victim are not dealt with adequately.

There is a dangerous myth that bullying is just part of growing up, that it is just 'quarrelling amongst peers', that young people should 'sort it out amongst themselves', and that leaving them to do so will strengthen their ability to deal with problems later in life. It is this myth which leads fathers to be angry with their sons for being 'wimpish' and not 'standing their ground' or 'fighting back', or leads mothers to believe that their daughters are just involved in 'bitchiness'.

To the contrary, bullying can involve physical assault, blackmail and extortion, systematic threat and intimidation, attack and theft, damage to possessions, assault on emotional and psychological well-being, and even the death of the victim who may be driven to suicide.

Bullying is also the problem that causes more agony in parents than any other school problem. Furthermore, being bullied rates amongst children's highest worries, and in one study of 4,000 children, 38% reported being bullied often enough or badly enough to be distressed.

When the effects of bullying were traced into adulthood, in one Swedish study, statistics showed that bullying in various forms accounted for from 200–400 suicides a year.

There have been some excellent Irish studies of bullying, one of which found that over one-third of Irish Primary School children reported being bullied. Over 43% reported occasionally bullying other children, and as many as 50% said that they had occasionally been bullied. Over one-fifth of children reported fear in coming to school because of bullying.

Internationally, the figures for serious ongoing bullying range from 5–10%, and Irish figures are high on this scale. Our tackling of the problem, therefore, has been less than excellent, and many parents, teachers or young people reading this chapter may have personally experienced the depression, misery and humiliation that bullying has caused to them or to those they know.

DEFINITIONS OF BULLYING

The most used definition of bullying is the Scandinavian one that 'bullying is long-standing violence, mental or physical, conducted by an individual or a group and directed against an individual who is not able to defend himself in the actual situation'. When this is translated into the reality of life for children it can mean many things:

- Being excluded from the group, who actively let you know that you are 'not wanted'.
- Having to bring protection money to school to keep you from being hit or kicked or threatened.
- Having to bring extra lunch or sweets to give to another child or children, so that you will be safe during school breaks.
- Trying on a hundred sets of clothes, hoping that what you wear will not be laughed at or smirked at.
- Never being picked for a team.
- Having to guard your possessions, or not bringing them with you because they will be broken, taken, or hidden.
- Hurrying into the presence of adults for safety.
- Having a desk slammed on your fingers, a pen poked in your eye, being bumped into, your lunch being stamped

on, your soft drink being spat into.

- Hiding in the toilets.
- Being called a 'tart', a 'slut', a 'scumbag', a 'dickhead', a 'sissy', a 'cry-baby', or having threats made against you.
- Having to 'watch your back'.
- Being whacked with a hockey stick or a hurley, having a tennis ball directed at you, being kicked with soccer boots, being punched in the rugby scrum.
- Believing that you are stupid, ugly, worthless, hated, a 'nerd', a 'wimp', a 'swot', a 'four-eyes', no good, unwanted, not fit to live.
- Believing that adults don't care, won't help, can't help, or that they blame you.
- Experiencing acute helplessness and hopelessness.
- Wishing your torturers were dead or, equally tragically, wishing that you were dead.

WHO ARE THE BULLIES?
Bullies are not always easy to detect, and because of the shame, secrecy and collusion that often surround bullying, many remain unidentified. Bullies may not always come to a teacher's attention because their class behaviour may be fine. The bully who is also disruptive, academically unable, emotionally disturbed, or challenging to a teacher is obviously more likely to be identified or observed.

The Anxious Bully
Such bullies tend to be emotionally distressed or disturbed and enact their distress in the hurting of another. If their upset is unattended to, bullying can be one form of expressing it. Often, bullies experience real self-hatred and feelings of inadequacy brought on by their own life experiences.

The Underachiever

An adolescent who is unable to keep up with studies, who feels stupid or frustrated, can easily resort to disruption in class and bullying outside of class, in order to hide inability and to gain status with peers. It is not uncommon for such adolescents to pretend that they don't care, to deride those who do, and to demonstrate strength either through physical or verbal cruelty.

In a study in England, it was found that bullies were more likely to be disruptive and hyperactive in class. It was also found, in Irish studies, that they often had lower IQs, with a higher proportion of both bullies and victims coming from the special and remedial classes. For this reason, it is very important that we do not put undue pressure to succeed on the adolescent.

The Bully with Problems at Home

Irish studies have found that as high a proportion as 70% of bullies come from problematic family backgrounds. Young people who are worried about their parents separating, who are in conflict with parents, who are feeling frightened or miserable, may easily divert their distress into bullying behaviour.

Parents' attitudes towards the adolescent and towards discipline (either too harsh or too permissive), have also been found to be an influence.

It has also been found that some parents of bullies could themselves be described as bullies. They behave in this way with their children, who then transfer their frustration on to the next weaker person.

Many bullies have been bullied by older or more powerful siblings, and the family ethos may be one of 'might is right'.

Young people who are not allowed to show or express their feelings, who are harshly or unjustly punished, who have been pressurised to succeed academically, who have been taught to be over-competitive or aggressive, or who have been abused in any way, often express these experiences by bulling.

OTHER CONTRIBUTORY FACTORS

The bully can be from any social group, as Irish and other studies have shown. Money and advantage are therefore neither protection against being bullied nor a guarantee that a child will not become a bully.

Many bullies are what are called 'bully victims'. They have been bullied themselves and try to recoup their sense of power and control over a person who cannot retaliate.

Bullies are more likely to be physically strong, to be angered easily, and to be unable to control their temper or their emotions. They are also more likely to have an accepting attitude towards violence. They may choose to watch and enjoy a greater number of violent films and videos, and they may enact such violence on others without any apparent appreciation of the suffering it causes. They may show few signs of guilt or remorse.

Bullies may be adolescents who have been overly criticised in childhood. They may have been physically assaulted (through violent discipline or corporal punishment), and they may have come to think that physical attack is an acceptable form of control.

Likewise, we as parents may have influenced their propensity to bully. When we make negative comments about social class, we invite them to believe that one group of people is superior to another. When we laugh at racial jokes, we invite them to prejudice. When we deride a religious belief, we lead them towards intolerance.

Furthermore, the parent who castigates a child invites other family members to do so. The teacher who ridicules a child invites the class to do so. Therefore, bullying may begin with adult behaviour and may arise in a society that tolerates violence at any level.

WHO ARE THE VICTIMS?

Victims may be intellectually more able or less able than peers. Victims may be tall or small, fat or slim, have wonderful or poor appearance, be materially advantaged or deprived. The sad reality of bullying is that almost anyone can be bullied.

Having said that, studies have attempted to look at the characteristics of victims in an effort to understand why one person, rather than another, becomes a victim. Two kinds of victims, 'passive' and 'provocative', have been identified.

The 'passive' victims are those who are unable to defend themselves, whereas the 'provocative' victims are those who irritate in some way, for example by being 'clumsy', or 'gauche', or having unusual hobbies.

Victims may also be different in some physical way, for example being overweight, having big ears, a big nose, a lack of personal hygiene, or, indeed, having anything different that may provide an opportunity for ridicule.

Victims of bullying may have problems with language and communication at a practical or functional level. They may be unable to appreciate jokes, fail to understand the rules of taking turns in conversation, or they may have difficulty reading facial expressions (their teachers, as well as their peers). They may also have problems respecting personal space, or they may have poor comprehension of conversations. As a result, they may be perceived as 'different', 'disruptive', or 'odd' and, therefore, are excluded by their peers.

Particularly intelligent or gifted adolescents can also be victims, because their ability attracts jealousy. They may antagonise their classmates by putting their hand up too frequently, or by being too enthusiastic about learning. They may also wish to discuss topics interesting to themselves, for example some new research findings, in contrast to topics of interest to others, for example the latest programmes on MTV or the problem of getting to the next disco.

Whatever the attributes of victims, many victims are chosen simply because the bully is looking for someone who can't oppose them. Furthermore, bullying is unacceptable and victims should never be blamed. Nobody invites abuse and it is never justified.

DIFFERENCES BETWEEN BOYS AND GIRLS?

Some studies have indicated that about twice as many boys as girls are bullies. However, other studies suggest that bullying amongst girls is under-reported and that, in fact, bullying by girls may be three times higher than bullying by boys. This may be because boys are more willing to admit to being bullies than girls. Certainly, in clinical encounters, girls often report a staggering degree of malicious, insidious, and acute verbal abuse and innuendo from other girls. Appearance, parents, social standing, boyfriends, possessions, ability, all are opportunities for ridicule, and appear to be the most common factors involved.

Research also indicates that a higher proportion of bullying amongst girls takes the form of teasing. In contrast, boys experience a higher proportion of physical bullying. Because bullying amongst girls often tends to take the more subversive forms of exclusion and taunting, there are less visible signs of the assault. However, both boys and girls feel equally rejected by bullying and it affects the happiness and self-esteem of both.

Amongst those who are bullied, there are also differences between boys and girls. Amongst the boys who are bullied, 88% report being bullied *only* by boys. Amongst girls who are bullied, 48% report being bullied by boys and 24% report being bullied by other girls.

HOW DO I KNOW IF MY TEENAGER IS BEING BULLIED?

Young people may not always directly communicate that they are being bullied. Often, they test the waters of adult understanding by dropping hints or by behavioural change. Sometimes, it is too hard for them to put words on the experience, particularly as being bullied lowers self-esteem and confidence to levels that make them uncertain about themselves and the reactions they will receive. Boys often feel ashamed in front of their fathers or afraid that they will be told that, 'No son of mine is a coward'. Likewise, girls are often ashamed that they have no friends and that they will be accused of 'bitching'.

The relationship you have with the young person is the most likely determinant of whether, and how, you will be told. Some young people, particularly adolescents, do not wish to worry their parents, or they believe that they should be able to handle the problem themselves now that they are growing up. Many fear that it will just make matters worse if their parents approach the bully, the bully's parents or the school. They fear that they might then have to suffer even greater persecution, as a result.

We need to be able to distinguish the signs of bullying from other adolescent signals and behaviours. The following are very common signals that an adolescent is being bullied:

- Excessive or sudden mood change, including change from contentment to unhappiness at school.
- Improvement in mood on days off school, at weekends and during holidays, and becoming notably stressed on Sunday evenings and before school.
- Deterioration in academic achievement.
- Dropping hints about their dislike of schoolmates, using phrases like 'She's a show off', or 'He's a pain', or even 'So and so doesn't like me'.

- Appearing to have no close friends at school, not being part of school groups, and not discussing positive events from their school life.

- Complaining of having nothing to do at break-time, or wanting to come home if school is close to home.

- Wanting to be driven to and from school, and becoming disproportionately distressed if this is not possible.

- Making negative remarks about themselves, including phrases such as, 'Nobody else thinks I'm pretty' or, 'You're the only one who thinks so', if you make a positive remark.

- Having too many unexplained cuts or bruises, experiencing too many 'accidents' at school. (Always get as much information as you can if you think that injuries are excessive.)

- Developing minor physical complaints or illnesses, particularly during the school week, and using them as an excuse to stay at home.

- Losing or forgetting too many possessions, and being angry or upset when questioned about them.

- Arriving home with too many damaged possessions, such as torn clothes or damaged books.

- Wanting to bring extra money or extra lunch to school, and being anxious if not allowed to do so.

WHAT CAN PARENTS DO?

At a general level, the better adolescents feel about themselves the less likely they are to be either bullies or victims. An adolescent who is being bullied needs all the support, love, validation and comfort you can provide. How we respond to an adolescent's disclosure of bullying is crucial. A poor response is just another rejection that could plunge the adolescent into hopelessness.

- Listen carefully to what the adolescent says and show that you are concerned, sympathetic and will help and defend them immediately.
- Do not say, 'Lets see if it blows over', because situations of real bullying usually get worse and the victim becomes more disempowered from seeking help.
- Never dismiss bullying as 'quarrelling' or 'bitching', and never accuse the adolescent of 'making excuses' for other problems.
- Let them know that they are not responsible for the bullying and that adults will solve the problem for them.
- Try to get the names of other young people who have been bullied and arrange to meet their parents. In this way, the victims will feel part of a group, and the parents can work with the school as a group.
- Work with the school to resolve the problem. If the school will not help, seriously consider removing the adolescent from the school.
- If you decide to remove your adolescent from the school, let the school authorities know why you are doing this and register a formal statement of complaint.
- In instances where the adolescent may be a 'provocative' victim, get social skills training or counselling to help them overcome the behaviour that might have provoked others to act against them.
- Never give your adolescent the message that they have to fight, or defend themselves, or defend their possessions.
- Avoid statements such as, 'How could you let them take your new bag, blazer, shoes, racquet from you?'
- Find every opportunity to praise, encourage and admire the adolescent. This will help them recover their self-esteem.
- If possible, plan some treats, buy new clothes, or organise

nice events to cheer up the adolescent.

HOW DO I KNOW IF MY TEENAGER IS A BULLY?

The following is a checklist of some symptoms and indicators you might like to consider:

- Is their self-esteem poor and their behaviour flamboyant?
- Have they shown a tendency to bully their brothers or sisters, or even their parents?
- Have they themselves been bullied by a brother or sister?
- Are they short-tempered, and do they react with extreme frustration or aggression if disciplined?
- Have they themselves had life experiences that may have made them feel bad about themselves, such as illness, a physical problem, or a problem with their appearance?
- Have they suddenly acquired possessions that you did not provide or that were not given to them by friends?
- Are there any particular family circumstances that might make them anxious, such as financial worries, marital difficulties, or serious illness?
- When they speak about other people at school, do they deride them on the basis of appearance or belief or possessions?
- Do they have an excessive interest in violence, and do they choose to watch such sequences excessively on television or video?
- Do they show little sensitivity towards other people?
- Have there been any complaints or suggestions that they may have bullied in the past?

If you find yourself answering *yes* to many of these questions, you may find that your adolescent is involved in bullying. If this is so, then your adolescent may need help with this behaviour.

WHAT CAN I DO IF MY TEENAGER IS A BULLY?

- Show absolute disapproval of the behaviour, *not* of the adolescent.
- Insist that the adolescent takes responsibility for any acts of bullying and apologises to the victim.
- Insist on repayment of money taken, and repair of goods damaged. It may be useful to lend the adolescent the money to do this and insist on repayment over time.
- Look for the meaning of the behaviour, including anxiety, inability at school, being bullied by others, etc.
- Promise your support to help them not to bully.
- Remember that they may need to change school and make a fresh start, particularly if they were in a 'mobbing' or 'bully' gang that has not been dismantled.
- Consider the family situations that might have caused the adolescent to bully. Ask them to explain to you if anything at home made them worried, such as jealousy of a brother or sister.
- If you think that not having enough of the popular adolescent 'gear' might have influenced them to bully, discuss what possessions are important to someone of their age and how they might earn enough to buy them either through rewards from home or from a job.
- Be sure that they don't have intellectual or academic difficulties that have not been identified or addressed.
- Reassure them of your continued love, help and concern, and that they can put what happened behind them.

WHAT CAN TEACHERS DO?

The bully has been found to be more accepted and more comfortable in some school climates than in others. In one study, a quarter of teachers thought it was sometimes best to ignore the problem. However, many teachers who do wish the problem to be addressed are sometimes left without a clear school policy on what action to take. At the end of the day, it is school policy which determines whether or not bullying is identified and tackled. Research does not show that class size or school size are directly related to the problem (although teachers may be under more pressure in such contexts). Therefore, it is the ethos of the school and the degree to which it tolerates or challenges bullying which are the most important factors.

A visible, documented, coordinated and publicly voiced bullying policy, understood by both parents and students, is essential in every school. Preferably, parents should be asked to give their understanding and consent to the procedures and processes that will occur where bullying is identified. The school should be aware of their legal and other rights when dealing with bullying, so that they are not intimidated either by the bullies themselves or by uncooperative parents. Teachers also need the reassurance and support of school principals and the Department of Education in serious cases.

In cases where bullying is suspected, schools should:

- Investigate the problem, and take reports of bullying seriously.
- Respond to every instance of bullying, however minor, and react immediately. 'Zero tolerance' is one of the best ways to tackle school bullying.
- Monitor the high-risk times for bullying, such as break-time, changing for sports, and the beginning and end of the school day.
- Monitor the physical locations in which bullying is more likely to occur, such as dark corridors, cloakrooms and changing-rooms, school yards, and bike sheds.
- Assign appropriate teachers to monitor bullying and to report on any observed incidents.

- Consciously comment on and reward kind, sensitive and non-bullying behaviour.
- Provide a presentation/lecture/video about bullying, which portrays the bully as a person with serious problems and inadequacies. This may help to dismantle any status the bully receives from his behaviour, and to deter potential bullies.
- Provide a support system for staff, and remember that many teachers are also bullied and are too ashamed to admit it.
- Where bullying is proved, reassure the victims that they are believed, that they will be helped and that the bullying will be stopped.
- In cases of serious bullying, suggest to the victim's parents that the victim should receive counselling.
- If the victim may have contributed to his victimisation through problems of personal hygiene, age-inappropriate clothes, annoying or disgusting behaviour, extreme fearfulness, elicit the parents' help to address these issues in order to protect their child in the future.
- Explore factors that may have caused the bully's behaviour in the first place, for example, abuse, inability to cope, parental harshness, or being bullied by others.
- Confront the *behaviour* of bullies, not the bullies themselves. Help them to discover other ways of coping with their problems.
- Where a group of bullies is involved, approach each one *individually* without any opportunity for them to meet with each other and devise a coherent excuse. Make sure that those who deny their participation know that you intend to pursue it until everyone involved has been identified.
- Bullying behaviour should be reacted to with clear, determined and unambiguous disdain.
- Insist that bullies repair or replace any damaged goods,

and that they apologise to the victim and plan restitution.

- Inform parents of both bully and victim of the problem, and seek their cooperation and attention.
- In situations where parents deny irrefutable bullying by their adolescent, insist on objective outside professional investigation and intervention.
- Where bullying is very severe and dangerous and the parents' reaction is violent, abusive and bullying, call the police.

Some schools may be reluctant to admit that bullying could occur in their school, on the basis that this may reflect badly on themselves. Schools need to remember that they are not responsible for the multitude of circumstances that cause bullying. However, whether or not bullying is facilitated or challenged in their school is up to them. Equally, schools need to feel supported at every level if they are to confront bullying. Such support can only come about through backup from the coordinated support of society and the Departments of Health, Education and Justice.

It must be remembered that bullying is not the 'rough and tumble', the boisterousness, or the occasional cruelty of childhood. It is a serious, physically threatening, and psychologically damaging occurrence that arrests adolescent development and causes untold problems to young people at a vulnerable life-cycle stage. You are right to be seriously worried about it, and if you are worried about your child being bullied, act immediately.

SHYNESS

ADOLESCENCE IS A TIME OF self-examination, social uncertainty and personal agonising, caused in part by the move from childhood into the complex world of adult communication.

Adolescence is also a time of change, forcing the young person to cope with new communicative and social skills, and also to adapt to a changing body which may feel uncomfortable and awkward.

The adolescent's new appearance can invite comments, and sexual remarks are particularly upsetting and confusing to the growing child. Patronising, derisory, and jocose remarks also do not help, and the fear of such comments can cause considerable problems.

If you add to this the sudden appearance of acne, the possible need for ungainly orthodontics, the teenage characteristics of profuse sweating, the voice breaking, or the body secretly menstruating, then you can understand why many teenagers suffer from acute embarrassment and anxiety.

Therefore, it is not surprising that shyness can often be disturbing and intense during the adolescent years. As adults, we can sometimes forget just how awkward are the behaviours and newly acquired social and communicative skills of adolescence.

We also forget that while many adapt to the new pressures with relative ease, there are some who do not. For these teenagers, the result may be shyness, leading to almost total avoidance of contact with others. Such avoidance is called 'social phobia', which is a severe and specific anxiety state.

The signs of social phobia in adolescents are as follows:

• Fear of meeting people, and avoiding social contact.

- Severe difficulties in making or in keeping friends.
- Being unable to make eye contact with others.
- Using excuses, especially illness, to avoid social encounters.
- Responding with anger or fear when encouraged to participate in normal social activities.
- Making self-deprecatory remarks about appearance, behaviour or clothes.
- Showing increased anxiety symptoms at the prospect of social encounters.
- Being forced to leave social situations abruptly because of discomfort, anxiety, or feelings of panic.
- Ruminating negatively on returning home from social events.
- Exhibiting self-doubt, including fears that people are laughing or sniggering in a derisory fashion.
- Showing signs of worry, apprehension, 'butterflies', perspiring, dry clammy hands, nausea, and dry-mouth while in company.
- Revealing signs of depression and an inability to cope.
- Avoiding school, or avoiding social activities in school.
- Using chemical substances, such as alcohol or drugs, before or after social events.

SOCIAL PHOBIA AND AGORAPHOBIA

Social phobia was first identified in the 1960s, and in recent years has come to be regarded as a prevalent and distressing form of anxiety. It is important to recognise that it is a distinct entity, and is not to be confused with agoraphobia.

Agoraphobics suffer a fear of impersonal public places, believing that if they enter them, they will suffer a panic attack. The agoraphobic dreads any encounter, such as walking on the street, shopping, or taking buses.

In contrast, the socially phobic person dreads *specific* encounters in which they are called upon to engage personally or socially. The primary focus for their fear is their dread of being humiliated, although they may also experience fear of panic in certain situations. What they do share, however, is the common experience of 'anticipatory anxiety', in other words the pressures that arise when thinking about, or anticipating, feared situations.

Research has shown that women with agoraphobia outnumber men in a ratio of four to one. In contrast, social phobia arises in equal proportions amongst boys and girls, with some studies suggesting an ever higher incidence in males. Interestingly, problems with shyness and social phobia can be observed in boys and girls as early as middle childhood (6–7 years) and extend into adolescence and beyond.

THE DIFFERENCE BETWEEN ADOLESCENT SHYNESS AND SOCIAL PHOBIA

In general terms, what distinguishes common adolescent sensitivity and shyness from severe social phobia, is the frequency, degree, duration, persistence, accumulation and severity of the symptoms.

Occasional sensitivity, discomfort, short-term curtailments of friendships and social activities, even blushing or social withdrawal, can be features of the normal process of adolescence. However, when the adolescent withdraws to a bedroom for prolonged periods, cuts off social contact, and exhibits other symptoms of social anxiety including anxiousness, being overwhelmed on social occasions, while also showing symptoms of depression and persistent avoidance, then it may be time to worry.

There is no easy demarcation point between safe levels of shyness and more worrying forms of persistent social phobia.

However, when it becomes clear that the adolescent's normal social activities are being restricted and curtailed to the detriment of their happiness and self-esteem, then a problem may exist.

WHAT CAN YOU DO TO HELP?

Acquiring social skills begins in infancy, and research studies indicate that the following are important determinants of how well an adolescent copes with social interactions:

- Having social role models to imitate, for example, parents, teachers, relatives, brothers and sisters.
- Being rewarded for good social behaviour.
- Having plenty of opportunities for play and for games.
- Being provided with the opportunity to practice social behaviour in many settings.
- Developing good language and communicative ability.
- Developing the intellectual capacity to understand another person's point of view.
- Having good health, so that illness does not arrest the normal developmental processes or cause school absences during which friendships may be lost or curtailed.
- Not being isolated from friendships during their upbringing.
- Not having parents who are excessively protective or anxious.
- Not having parents who are socially uncomfortable.

By the time the child reaches adolescence, there are also many steps to be taken in overcoming their problems with shyness:

- Do not set your expectations too high by presuming that your adolescent is able to hold fluent, comfortable conversations with your adult friends, when they are simply not able to do so. Unobtrusively assist them in these encounters.

- Do not confuse shyness with 'reserve', and try not to demand that they be effusive in social interactions. We all have a right to our own personality.
- Teach them the appropriate social greetings and skills, such as when to shake hands, how to address people, how to write 'Thank you' letters, etc.
- Don't force adolescents to go to functions or to participate in activities they are not yet ready for. Saying, 'Perhaps you might like to go the next time' is encouraging.
- Allow young people to bring their friends to the house, and be warm and friendly to them when they arrive.
- Never ridicule adolescents in front of their friends. If you are angry with your child for some reason, wait until the friends have gone and then discuss your feelings.
- Never make comments on an adolescent's physical appearance to others, particularly regarding the physical signs of growing up. Adolescents can experience this as humiliating, hurtful, and even sexually abusive.
- Try not to patronise young people, and avoid making jokes at their expense.
- Restrain yourself from castigating their choice of clothes. If they are inappropriate to the point of being unsafe, discuss your concern with your child.
- Never compare your adolescent to friends or siblings who are socially more skilled. None of us likes to be told we are less able than others.
- Provide as many opportunities as you can afford to develop their social skills and confidence, such as bringing them to restaurants and allowing them to choose and to order for themselves.

- Provide them with as many opportunities as possible to expand their general knowledge, so that they will not feel ignorant in social conversations.
- Allow them to watch programmes like 'Top of the Pops' or some of the more acceptable 'soaps' if that is what their peers will be discussing the next day in school.
- Within reason, provide them with the age-appropriate clothes that their friends are wearing, so that they will not feel different.
- Make sure they have enough pocket-money, so that they are not embarrassed in front of others.
- Allow them to have opinions that are different to yours.
- Acknowledge that they have something to say and something to teach us. Thank them when they impart information or ideas of their own.
- Invite your friends into the home so that they can observe social exchanges.
- Emphasise that feeling shy and uncertain amongst people their age is normal, and suggest that they observe others rather than observe themselves.
- Try to be comfortable about their friendships with other boys and girls, in particular their friendships with members of the opposite sex.
- Provide the opportunity or money for age-appropriate hairstyles, the cosmetics they require, or any aids to their appearance and presentation that will help their self-esteem.
- If they have a physical blemish, such as a birthmark, get professional advice and consider cosmetic camouflage.
- Attend to any difficulties they may have, such as stuttering, stammering or lisping. Bring them to an appropriate speech and language therapist.
- If you think that they have a problem in either expressing

themselves or in comprehension of language, consult a language therapist. (Research shows that poor processing of social cues can lead to social phobia.)

- Find every opportunity to admire, praise, encourage, and show concern for the adolescent.

PROFESSIONAL TREATMENT

The traditional treatment for phobias has been to help people to gradually confront the feared object or situation until the anxiety abates. This is done by progressively exposing, and thereby desensitising, the person to their fear. This approach has proven to be highly successful in the treatment of many common phobias, such as the fear of spiders or the fear of open spaces.

Unfortunately, when people with social phobia have been exposed to the object of their fear (social situations), it has been found that their problems do not get better. Indeed, the more a person tries to cope with social situations, the greater their self-consciousness, self-monitoring, and the greater their sense of foolishness.

This leads to the development of strategies or 'safety behaviours', such as avoiding eye contact, covering the mouth, or bringing their hair down over the face. In this way, social phobics hope that their anxiety will not be recognised by others.

This intensive preoccupation with what they are doing leads them not to observe others, and can cause them to focus exclusively on themselves and their perceived inadequacies. By dwelling in this way on the negative factors, their anxiety is heightened for the next social encounter.

To cope with these difficulties, researchers at Warnford Hospital, University of Oxford, have developed a new and radically different approach to treatment. This approach involves helping the person to review social interactions that have made them anxious, and to examine the image they have of themselves in social situations.

Treatment also involves role-playing without using safety behaviours, and video feedback to show the positive effects of dropping the safety behaviours. The person is also asked to look at how others have responded to them rather than concentrating on how they feel about themselves. Furthermore, they are helped to avoid ruminating after social events, and they are helped to challenge their dysfunctional social assumptions.

The results of this new form of treatment have been encouraging, showing greater success rates than any of the other psychological treatments used to date. Above all, this new development has highlighted the fact that extreme shyness is a special and a particular type of phobia, which requires specialised help to overcome the problem and to help the adolescent recover self-esteem and confidence during the teenage years.

The sad fact is that the majority of people presenting for treatment for social phobia do so as adults, after many years of suffering. As teenagers, many social phobics may have had their behaviour misattributed to adolescent awkwardness or moodiness. It is, therefore, essential to monitor carefully any symptoms of chronic social withdrawal or of inability to communicate or converse in social settings, and to ensure, where such cases persist, that professional advice is sought.

EATING PROBLEMS

DURING CHILDHOOD, FOOD IS USUALLY eaten with parents, and directly chosen and provided by them. This changes in adolescence, as young people develop independence and begin to exercise their 'right to choose'.

During adolescence, young people are exposed to considerable pressure from media advertising to buy certain foods. Furthermore, at this stage, adolescents require vast intakes of food to meet their energy needs and to accommodate the 'growth spurt'.

The attitudes of parents and peers towards body shape and size will also influence the adolescent's body-image. Since body-image is often bound up with eating, both boys and girls may decide that what they eat, or how much they eat, will help to determine the way they look.

This is a time when young people may decide that they can reject eating or eat to excess. Such decisions may either be construed as a problem or they may simply reflect one of the struggles for independence in a teenager's life. In either case, the symptoms are likely to be broadly the same, and this fact can be highly confusing to parents who are observing the changing behavioural patterns of their adolescent child.

Before progressing to the serious problems that can develop, it is worth examining what these initial eating patterns might be:

- Showing an excessive enjoyment of hamburgers, chips, fried chicken, kebabs, pizzas, milk-shakes, doughnuts, hot-dogs, battered sausages.
- Overindulging in fatty, high-calorie, take-away foods.
- Snacking on crisps, peanuts, chocolate, biscuits, sweets,

67

along with sugar-rich and salty foods.
- Constantly complaining about being 'hungry', 'starving', or 'dying of hunger'.
- Taking frequent intervals from study to consume snacks, and eating sweets and chocolate while studying.
- Excessively eating 'starchy' or 'sweet' foods while watching television. Don't forget that young people may watch many hours of television each day.
- Eating and drinking rapidly. Stuffing food, and gulping drinks.
- Showing an obsessive interest in diets and dieting, and spending a lot of money on magazines containing articles on food or diets.
- Resenting parental pressure to eat particular foods, and reacting strongly to the parents' suggestions.
- Becoming excessively concerned about the links between food and health. Additionally, becoming excessively aware of the connection between food, weight, and body-image.
- Becoming overly-embarrassed by their parents' appearance, in particular if parents are fat.
- Tending to eat more at times of stress, or eating substantially more or less when feeling 'down'.
- Comforting themselves with cakes, biscuits, and other sugary foods.

OVEREATING

Obesity is normally defined as weighing more than 20% over the normal bodily requirements. Some studies suggest that the causes can originate in early life, when over-nutrition can produce excessive fat cells which remain throughout the later years.

Other studies point to hereditary factors, and still others investigate metabolic functioning, which determines the relationship between nutritional input and energy output.

Many more studies suggest that environmental factors can influence overweight, in particular patterns of family eating and attitudes towards exercise. Finally, additional studies suggest that some individuals may lack the ability to respond to internal body cues, and are therefore unable to determine that they have eaten sufficiently or in the required amounts.

There are many other factors which influence overeating, including the following:

- Many high-calorie, fatty or sugary foods are pleasurable to eat, and attractive in taste, texture and presentation. The eating of these foods can, therefore, be a highly enjoyable experience.
- Many sweet or 'filling' foods can act as a comfort, filling a gap in adolescents' lives at times when they feel unhappy or rejected.
- Parents may set a pattern for overeating in early childhood by using certain foods for reward or punishment, and by connecting these foods with the feeling of being loved or cared for.
- Parents may also shape an adolescent's attitude to food by insisting that certain foods *have* to be eaten, that certain quantities *must* be consumed, and that certain body weights or levels of food intake are necessary.
- Patterns of overeating can begin during the adolescent 'growth spurt', which takes place in early adolescence. These unhealthy patterns of eating may cause weight-gain in later adolescent years.

SYMPTOMS OF OVEREATING

Parents who are concerned that an adolescent is overeating may like to look out for the following signs:

- Finding it hard to resist foods, and always seeking an extra helping when other family members are satisfied.
- Rummaging in cupboards for cakes and biscuits, and 'demolishing' an entire cake or a full packet of biscuits at one sitting.
- Showing a preference for 'junk' food, to the exclusion of other more healthy or nutritious foods.
- Becoming upset about being overweight and feeling helpless to do anything about it.
- Deciding that excess weight is so great that it is pointless trying to reduce it.
- Feeling bad about eating too much, and eating more to compensate for the guilt.
- Going on binges, especially binges of high-fat foods.
- Believing that personal problems stem from being overweight, and imagining that if they were slim those problems wouldn't exist.
- Eating excessively one day, and then compensating by eating nothing at all on the next day.
- Finding that food relieves unhappiness, loneliness and feelings of low self-esteem.
- Feeling an emotional emptiness regardless of how full the stomach may be.
- Always feeling hungry, and always having the urge to eat.
- Looking forward to food, rushing home for meals, eating chocolate on the way, and thinking incessantly about the next meal or treat.
- Worrying that being overweight will result in the opposite sex becoming repelled. As a result, avoiding locations for meeting the opposite sex, such as discos, sports or social outings.
- Avoiding exercise, as weight becomes an embarrassment or physically taxing. Being unable to exercise vigorously.

- Seeking food or sweets as a reward for good behaviour.
- Hiding the amounts being eaten, and preferring to eat alone.
- Storing food for later consumption, and feeling anxious if adequate food supplies are not available.
- 'Needing' food, and if preferred foods are not available eating anything that is to hand.
- Being ridiculed by friends or classmates, and perhaps becoming a victim of bullying.
- Engaging in bullying behaviour as an expression of feelings of inadequacy.
- Making self-deprecatory remarks, telling jokes about 'fat' people, or pretending to find being overweight amusing.
- Finding that eating and weight are out of control, and trying 'emergency' weight-reduction measures, such as using laxatives or short-term starving.
- Using vomiting as a way of removing meals from the stomach, and doing so on a very regular basis. Feeling compelled to induce vomiting immediately after a meal.
- Feeling tense, ashamed and guilty, when eating or having eaten.

UNDEREATING

Young people are aware of the control they have over their own lives, and eating can become a primary battleground for control. The image of the child in the high-chair, with lips pursed and head averted, while the parent sits, with spoon in hand, giving words of encouragement, is a familiar one to all of us.

By the time the child reaches adolescence they have also become conscious of the need to look 'healthy', and are influenced in this awareness by the many media images that promote slimness. They may observe, with envy, the excessive slimness of models, television personalities and film stars. They listen to the negative messages that are communicated about the over-eater. They compare their own figures with the 'ideal' and are often disappointed with the comparison.

This may lead young people to engage in the following behaviours:

- Becoming conscious of food, aware of foods that are described as 'fattening', and avoiding such foods.
- Weighing themselves constantly, and comparing their weight with other friends, or keeping records of changes and variations in weight.
- Remarking on their own body weight. Comments may be negative, such as, 'I'm too fat', or 'I have to watch my weight'.
- Watching their own intake of food, and refusing food because of weight concerns.
- Becoming extremely embarrassed if they cannot fit into the same size clothes as friends.
- Frequently observing themselves in the mirror, and complaining about the size of thighs, tummies and bottoms.
- Remarking on their weight to parents, and showing upset that they are not the same as their friends.
- Asking parents to cook different foods, 'drying' fried food with absorbent paper, being conscious of not eating foods that may be fattening.
- Envying friends who seem to be able to eat what they like without putting on weight, and copying their friends' eating patterns.
- Wearing clothes that conceal body parts, such as breasts, hips, the tummy, midriff, or legs.
- Being embarrassed to undress for games in school, because of the shame of revealing an imperfect physique.
- Trying out diets, calorie counting, and excessively monit-

oring food intake.
- Thinking incessantly about food, and worrying about food consumption.

DANGEROUS UNDEREATING PROBLEMS

At this stage, the young person is moving from dissatisfaction with self and with body-image and is beginning to enter into a series of behaviours that are bound up with serious undereating. The adolescent is becoming preoccupied with food, and this preoccupation may be affecting their normal development.

If you are anxious that your child falls into this bracket, you should look out for the following significant signs:

- Hiding loss of weight by wearing clothes that conceal.
- Cooking for others but not partaking in the meal that has been prepared.
- Becoming preoccupied with the 'perfect' body, and a general striving for perfection.
- Distorting and exaggerating true weight and size. Refusing to accept the assurances of others (often parents), or becoming angry if they persist in their view.
- Pretending to eat by putting tiny pieces into the mouth, hoping that the parents won't notice. Eating food very slowly and meticulously.
- Shuffling food around the plate, or compressing the food to make it look as if more has been consumed.
- Telling lies about eating. Pretending to friends that they have eaten at home. Pretending at home that they have eaten with friends.
- Exercising with the sole intention of reducing body fat, and developing an increasing preoccupation with exercise.
- Experiencing the body as 'separate', or not part of oneself.

- Feeling 'full', having eaten very little food.
- Experiencing excessive mood swings, and being afraid to express emotions.
- Experiencing poor self-esteem, and feeling no longer in control.
- Wanting to be someone else, and thinking that the answer lies in slimness.
- Equating slimness with success, and fatness with failure.
- Discarding the packed lunch on the way to school, or feeding the family pet under the table at mealtimes.
- Withdrawing from others, becoming anxious, lonely and uncertain, and becoming increasingly ruminative about what has been eaten during the day.
- Occasionally 'bingeing', which is normally followed by enormous guilt. Food may be regurgitated following a binge.
- Taking laxatives or enemas to remove food from the body.
- Feeling anxious at the slightest increase in weight.
- Finding that weight loss has led to the cessation of menstruation (periods).
- Feeling intense shame or guilt when eating or having eaten.

WHAT CAN A PARENT DO?

It is important that significant eating problems are tackled with urgency and understanding. This is necessary not only to ensure that the problem is contained at an early stage, but also to ensure that the adolescent does not suffer from the short-term nutritional, psychological, or medical effects of poor eating habits.

It is important for parents to know how to minimise the risk of adolescents encountering eating problems, and the following suggestions may be of use:

- Avoid using food to reward or to punish.
- Avoid family disagreements at mealtimes. If upset or criticism are associated with eating, the risk of developing eating problems is increased.
- Do not show anger if school lunches are brought home uneaten. If you express anger, they are likely to get thrown away the next time around. Instead, inquire if there is an alternative lunch they would like.
- Allow the young person some choice of foods at mealtimes. We all have certain foods we do not like.
- Never force an adolescent to eat a food they find repulsive.
- Prepare healthy snacks, including cut carrots, apples and oranges. These may be just as tempting to the adolescent as biscuits or sweets. Sometimes, laziness is the cause of an adolescent choosing a biscuit instead of peeling an orange.
- Allow some independence in the purchase of food, and encourage the adolescent to accompany you when shopping.
- Try to vary your recipes, and select recipes that are attractive to your child.
- Consider providing a low-fat, low-salt diet, as this has been linked to good health. Balance is everything.
- Recognise that adolescents require more food during the 'growth spurt'. Remarks such as, 'You are eating us out of house and home' are not helpful at this time.
- Take young people out to a restaurant and allow them to choose for themselves what they would like to eat.
- Never remark on overweight, either in the adolescent, in yourself, or in others. When possible, show that you do not admire excessive slimness.
- Try not to compare the young person's physique with the physique of a brother or sister.
- Never make jokes about fatness or fat people.
- Avoid negative comment on the physical and sexual de-

velopment of the adolescent, particularly the sexual characteristics.

- Reassure an adolescent who physically matures either early or late that such variation is normal.
- Taking a walk together may help the adolescent to exercise. It may also allow them the opportunity to discuss problems with you when alone.
- Remember the old but useful maxim, 'Eat like a king in the morning, a prince at noon and a pauper in the evening'. Try to encourage the young person to start the day with a good breakfast and keep night-time snacks as light as possible.
- Try not to make an issue about what the adolescent eats or does not eat. Most bodies are programmed to eat what they require.
- Be vigilant for any causes of stress or unhappiness in the young person's life, and provide as much help as you can.

EATING DISORDERS: ANOREXIA NERVOSA AND BULIMIA

Some of the symptoms listed above can culminate in severe eating disorders, such as anorexia nervosa and bulimia. These are very serious disorders and the treatments are highly specific.

In the event of your teenager showing signs of any of these disorders, seek *immediate* medical and psychiatric intervention. Such disorders require highly specialised care.

Anorexia nervosa is essentially characterised by self-induced weight loss through avoiding food. It can involve food avoidance to the point of starvation. It usually involves complex psychological disturbance. Anorexia nervosa is also most commonly associated with adolescent girls, with an estimated 90% of sufferers being female.

Anorexia nervosa

Problems associated with anorexia nervosa include:

- A striving for perfection.
- An obsessional need to be in control of oneself and one's life.
- Family patterns of discipline that may be harsh or exacting, and with high expectations.
- A delusional disturbance in body-image.
- A pattern of increasing manipulation, secrecy and deception about food intake. Hiding weight loss by putting weights in the pocket, or drinking water before being weighed are not uncommon practices. In this way, the sufferer hopes to deceive those who are monitoring the condition.
- Avoidance of entering womanhood. It is often suggested that sexual abuse may be part of the history of many young people with this condition. Retaining a childlike body weight and appearance may be perceived as protective by a young person in this situation.
- Behaviours such as severe purging, the use of laxatives, and vomiting may arise.
- Serious medical complications that can lead to death.
- Death by suicide (estimated to occur in approximately 5% of cases).

Bulimia

Bulimia is characterised by binge-eating followed by purging of the food. The compulsion to eat is strong, and large quantities of food are ingested. Such binges can occur frequently, ranging from several times a week to, in some cases, many times a day.

Bulimia is a condition that is more commonly associated with older adolescents and young adults, especially females.

Bulimia may develop on its own, but some people suffering with anorexia nervosa also develop symptoms of bulimia. Again, this is a condition that requires specialist psychiatric help.

Problems associated with the condition include:

- Poor self-esteem, eating for comfort or to fill the 'emptiness' of life, or eating to compensate for emotional distress.
- Enormous secrecy with regard to food. Deception and manipulation may be observed.
- A strong compulsion to eat, and the ingestion of large quantities of food in a 'binge'. Ingesting such quantities frequently, and for a prolonged period, determines whether or not a person is bulimic.
- Suffering secretly for a long time before seeking help (the average time is reported to be as much as five to six years).

Adolescence is a time of preoccupation with physical appearance, and the rapid and dramatic physical and sexual changes that occur during puberty inevitably make adolescents conscious of how they look.

It is important that the adolescent's concept of their appearance and their sense of self-image should be finely tuned. If not, the danger exists that poor eating patterns may escalate into problematic conditions, including anorexia nervosa, bulimia, binge-eating, and problems of obesity.

At the end of the day, the important thing is to treat eating patterns with tolerance and flexibility. As long as basic nutritional requirements are ingested, there is little to fear. But in the event that serious symptoms develop, it cannot be overstressed that eating problems and eating disorders can be complicated to resolve. In such an event, it is imperative to get urgent medical care.

TEENAGE DRINKING

TEENAGERS DRINK AT AN EXTRAORDINARY young age. The average child who starts to drink will do so by the age of 12. This is an astonishingly early entry into the world of alcohol.

Regardless of what leads to that initial drink, it is the first encounter with a potent substance called 'alcohol', a drug that is not only potentially toxic but also addictive or even fatal.

There has been a reported 360% increase, in just over a decade, in the number of teenagers being treated for alcohol disorders in psychiatric hospitals.

In a study of Dublin schoolchildren, it was found that 38% of those aged 13–17 years had been drunk on at least one occasion. In a further survey by St John of God Hospital, in County Dublin, which examined 14–17 year olds, 83% of those surveyed had used alcohol.

In real terms, this means that if your child is in a class of 30 pupils, 11 will have already been drunk at least once, and 25 of those classmates will have tasted drink in some form or other.

THE CATEGORIES OF TEENAGE DRINKING

- *The experimenters*. These are young people who sample drink once or twice as part of the adolescent process of experimentation. They may or may not get drunk, but the experiment is not repeated.
- *The participators*. This category consists of teenagers who take a 'nip' occasionally, especially when in the company of friends who are drinking.
- *The alcohol users*. These are the regular alcohol imbibers, who consume drink either socially or to escape worries. The tolerance to drink and the frequency of use will tend to slowly increase in this category. This type of alcohol con-

sumption may be described as *the pre-alcoholic phase.*

- *The alcohol abusers.* These are the regular drinkers for whom drink and getting drunk has become part of their lives. They may not have developed a dependence, but they may have taken some critical steps on the path to alcoholism. This phase is known as *initial alcoholism* and is characterised by the consumption of more drink per swallow and the imbibing of drinks with a higher alcohol content. There may also be loss of self-esteem and occasional blackouts.

- *The alcohol dependants.* This is known as *the chronic stage,* where the teenager requires alcohol on a daily basis and has developed a tolerance and a dependence that interferes with their physical, psychological and social development. During this stage, there may be daytime drinking, loss of control over alcohol, inadequate nourishment, poor judgement and thinking, along with a defensive attitude being portrayed by the adolescent.

Most parents may not be overly worried if their adolescent falls into the first two categories; the once-off experiment or the irregular trials are not too disturbing. Indeed, the thrill of testing the limits and experimenting with alcohol is part of the process by which an adolescent progresses to adulthood. For most teenagers, the only consequences are likely to be a very sore head, a feeling of nausea and a strong sense of regret.

However, others teenagers may progress to a lifelong problem with alcohol. It is for this reason that we, as adults, need to understand what causes alcohol abuse and the problems of tolerance and dependence.

WHY DO TEENAGERS DRINK?
There are many possible explanations for the early entry by adolescents into the world of drink. The following is a list of

some of those reasons:

- The attraction to drink as a sign of maturity.
- Emulating parents' drinking habits, and being influenced by general attitudes towards alcohol.
- Peer pressure, and the need to boost self-esteem by showing that you are part of the crowd.
- For boys the need to be 'macho', and for girls the need to portray sophistication.
- Using alcohol to overcome shyness and to mask inhibitions.
- Using alcohol to break down barriers between boys and girls at a time of great uncertainty about encounters with the opposite sex.
- Masking depression, and using alcohol to escape from the constraints of everyday life.
- Challenging the authority of parents, or signalling to parents that help is required.
- Using alcohol as an aid to coping with the pressures of school and everyday life.
- Drinking because they are bored, or cut off from other social, sporting or entertainment activities.
- Consuming alcohol because they have lost control over the substance.

WHERE DO ADOLESCENTS GET DRINK?

Young people have always been particularly inventive and creative in obtaining that which is vehemently denied. Drink is no exception. The adolescent who wants to drink can get alcohol in the following ways:

- Stealing it from home. (It is advisable that drink is not too visible or accessible in the home.)

- Stealing it from shops and off-licences. (Thereby introducing the adolescent to other dangerous activities.)
- Acquiring alcohol from friends.
- Exchanging possessions for drink.
- Using pocket-money or lunch money to purchase supplies.
- Asking older friends to purchase alcohol for them.
- Drinking in pubs while still under-age.

HOW WILL I RECOGNISE A TEENAGE DRINK PROBLEM?

You may not know if your child has tasted drink once or twice, or even if they have got drunk on one or two occasions. However, if your adolescent comes home drunk, you need to determine whether this is a once-off experiment or whether it is simply the first time you have observed part of a sequence.

There are many clear signs to observe if your teenager is drinking to excess:

- Coming home drunk.
- Smelling of alcohol, or leaving the odours of alcohol on clothes or pillows.
- Leaving odours of vomit in bedrooms.
- Taking preparations after a night out, particularly preparations for headaches.
- Appearing with bloodshot eyes, and complaining of general fragility.
- Wanting to stay over with friends, or to remain out excessively late.
- Seeking extra money when going out with friends.
- Showing signs of secretiveness or deception, and expressing anger when found to be lying.
- Withdrawing from family activities, and showing a marked disimprovement at school.
- Exhibiting arrogant and grandiose behaviour, along with a

82

sharp change in moods.

- Returning home with unexplained cuts or bruises, which might suggest an alcohol-related fight.
- Changing eating habits, and a notable disinterest in food.
- Blaming others for everything that goes wrong, and not connecting behaviour problems to alcohol.

THE EFFECTS OF ALCOHOL

Because the subject of drink is often treated as taboo, adolescents may be left with little information about the substance they are experimenting with. However, teenagers need to know the physiological and psychological effects of drink and the dangers that intoxication can cause to the body.

They also need to know the dangers of getting drunk, passing out, vomiting, choking, the risk of causing accidents, or being taken advantage of by others.

Adolescents should, therefore, be armed with the following information:

- Alcohol primarily affects the adolescent's central nervous system. While many people think of alcohol as a stimulant which increases excitement, it is, in fact, a depressant which slows down or depresses many activities in the brain.
- The short-term effects of excessive drinking are obvious, with alcohol being absorbed very quickly into the bloodstream and beginning to have an effect within approximately ten minutes.
- As the number of drinks increases, there is loss of coordination and deterioration in mental alertness, leading to staggering, slurred speech and the irrational, inane, maudlin, aggressive or grandiose pronouncements of the person who is drunk.
- Alcohol is measured in units. One unit of alcohol is approxi-

mately equal to one glass of wine, one glass of sherry, a small whiskey, or one-half of a pint of ordinary beer.

- Cans of beer (so favoured by adolescents) can range from 2–5 units depending on strength. A pint of cider has approximately 3 units. Young adolescents often drink flagons of cider because they are cheap, and each flagon contains about 10 units.

- Even small amounts of alcohol can increase the risk of accidents. At 4 units, the risk of accident is increased by a multiple of ten. At 6 units, it is increased by a multiple of 40. These levels of consumption may lead to impulsiveness, anti-social behaviour, risk-taking, or poor judgement.

- More young deaths are reportedly caused each year by alcohol-related accidents than by accidents related to the consumption of all other drugs.

FACTORS DETERMINING THE EFFECTS OF DRINK

The effects of alcohol on adolescents will depend on a number of factors, including the following:

- When the young person last ate some food. (Drink is more rapidly absorbed by an empty stomach.)

- Body build and weight, which will vary according to the age and stage of growth of the adolescent. (This is what makes drinking by very young 10–12 year olds so dangerous and more likely to lead to intoxication.)

- The amount of alcohol imbibed, and the extent to which drinks have been mixed.

- How quickly the alcohol has been drunk. (Young adolescents may not be aware that alcohol needs to be drunk more slowly than other beverages.)

- The individual's tolerance to drink. (This will depend on the regularity of use over time.)

- Whether other substances have been consumed by the adolescent. (Young people who combine alcohol and other drugs are taking considerable risks.)
- The psychological disposition of the adolescent. (Since adolescence is a time of great emotional instability, the level of maturity of the drinker can be significant.)

THE LONG-TERM EFFECTS OF DRINKING

There are many alarming long-term effects of alcohol abuse, including the following:

- Prolonged heavy drinking in alcoholic men can result in the failure of the liver to suppress female sex hormones. This leads to loss of body hair, increase in voice pitch, enlargement of the breasts (called gynaecomastia), and atrophy of the testicles.
- Gastric problems are very common in alcoholism, and peptic ulceration may eventually result.
- Cirrhosis of the liver, which is a chronic inflammatory disease, will develop in approximately 10% of alcoholics.
- Obesity may result from excessive alcohol consumption. Alcohol consumption provides calories but little nourishment. The 'beer belly' is a familiar sign of over-drinking.
- Alcohol can contribute to cancers, pancreatic disease, and also heart disease (alcoholic cardiomyopathy).
- Vomiting, hallucinations, unconsciousness, or even death can occur if alcohol is consumed in conjunction with other drugs. Passing out and vomiting may occur while asleep, and choking on the vomit is not uncommon.
- There is a higher risk of death from suicide, drug overdose, and other medical problems among those who abuse alcohol.
- Serious long-term abuse can lead to permanent brain-

damage. An alcohol-related condition called *Wernickes' encephalopathy* is characterised by confusion, loss of memory and degeneration of nerves, leading to many problems including the wasting of some muscles.

- Long-term abuse can further result in a condition called *Korsakoff's psychosis*. This involves memory loss, disorientation, and loss of insight.
- Alcohol can cause anxiety, self-deception, depression, guilt, and remorse. Indeed, alcohol-related pathological jealousy may lead to acts of extreme violence, including murder.
- Withdrawal can include tremulousness, or 'the shakes', which may cause alcoholics to drink more in order to stop their hands from shaking. This difficulty in coordination can make it difficult to lift even a glass of alcohol to the lips.
- In withdrawal, alcoholics can experience acute and chronic visual and auditory hallucinations. This is referred to as the 'DTs', or *Delirium Tremens*.
- Convulsions may occur within one to two days of withdrawal from alcohol.
- When chronic alcoholics give up drink, they can face difficult and life-long efforts to retain sobriety.

OTHER EFFECTS OF ALCOHOL CONSUMPTION
Research studies show that young people who abuse alcohol are more likely to:

- Abuse other substances.
- Engage in precocious sexual activity.
- Experience problems at school, and manifest lower motivation towards education.
- Be at greater risk of teenage pregnancy.
- Come into contact with the Gardaí due to alcohol-related vandalism and violence.

- Drop out of school.
- Cope poorly with difficulties in their lives.
- Be at greater risk of suicide.
- Be in greater conflict with parents and authority in general.
- Feel more vulnerable to peer pressure.

DIFFERENCES BETWEEN BOYS AND GIRLS

There are many differences in the effects of alcohol on boys and girls, including the following:

- Equivalent amounts of alcohol will have a greater effect on girls than on boys. The reason for this is that alcohol is diluted in the male body to a greater extent than in the female body.
- Women generally weigh less than men, with the result that there are higher concentrations of alcohol in females than in males.
- If girls drink alcohol in the same amounts as men, alcohol-related problems will develop at a faster rate.
- Women are more likely to develop the type of cirrhosis linked to alcoholism than men.
- Young men are more likely than women to develop pancreatitis, which is often associated with bout drinking.
- Girls are less able physically to defend themselves if they become involved with a group who react aggressively or violently under the influence of alcohol.
- Drinking removes inhibitions, with the result that both boys and girls may engage in sexual behaviours that they would not consider appropriate when sober. For girls, however, this carries all the dangers of teenage pregnancy, with the accompanying problems that are associated with it.

HOW CAN YOU HELP YOUR TEENAGER?

Many parents complain that they are unable to confront teenage drinking. They feel helpless to prevent their child from becoming involved and to stop them if they do so.

In fact, parents have far more power in this process than they think, and the following guidelines may be helpful:

- Your own behaviour and attitudes in relation to drink are the most important determinants as to whether or not your child will drink. The model you present to the adolescent is more powerful than any peer pressure they might experience.
- If alcohol is used moderately in the home, brought out for special occasions, or if parents are seen to drink the odd glass of wine with a meal, this is a powerful example for the growing adolescent to emulate.
- Where family problems exist, young people should see parents reach for the kettle, not the bottle. This shows that alcohol is *never* a solution to anything.
- Young people who, at an early age, are introduced to sport and to role models in sport (who tend not to drink) will emulate them. Emphasise that alcohol and strength, good health and physique do not go together.
- From an early age, be derisory about those who drink and drive, and never let your children see you do so.
- It is advised not to speak with amusement about drunkenness, nor to tell 'amusing' stories about things people did when drunk. It is useful if drunk behaviour is always presented in a negative light.
- When speaking about the dangers of alcohol, address the dangers to everyone, not just to young people. Adolescents will see it as unfair if you speak as if only young people have a problem with alcohol.

- Young people need to know about the physiological and psychological dangers of drink, and it is up to you to explain them. (See earlier list.)
- A parent should never buy a drink for an underage person in a pub. Remember that only those over 18 are entitled in law to purchase a drink or have drink purchased for them in a pub.
- Parents may make their own choice about whether or not to allow adolescents to drink, on occasions. For example, a sip of champagne at a wedding or christening, or a glass of wine at Christmas, can be useful ways to demystify drink.
- Research suggests that a message of 'don't touch at all' is not as helpful as a message of 'use moderately', when adolescents reach drinking age.
- Teach adolescents the legal position regarding drink:
    1) It is illegal to give alcohol to a child under 5 years. 2) Under 15 years, you are legally allowed into a pub in the company of a parent or guardian but not permitted to buy or consume alcohol. 3) Over 15 years, you are legally allowed into a pub on your own but not permitted to buy or consume alcohol. 4) Under 18 years of age, it is an offence to be in possession of alcohol or to consume it in *any* public place. 5) It is an offence to buy, or try to buy, drink under 18 years of age. 6) Buying drink for a minor is an offence. 7) It is an offence to drive under the influence of drink. 8) Advertisements for alcohol must use models aged 25 or over.
- Explain the physiological reasons why alcohol is not allowed for the very young rather than saying, 'You're not old enough to drink'.
- Emphasise health risks, problems with skin, weight and appearance, the effects on schoolwork, and the impact of alcohol in reducing fitness and causing illness.

- Explain about any family predisposition to alcohol and the associated dangers of drinking.
- Emphasise 'safety' rather than 'morality'. This may be more meaningful to the adolescent, who will be likely to appreciate your concerns.
- Research suggests that information about alcohol has a positive effect on the adolescent, and that it is more useful when provided slowly over a period of time.
- Giving 'hot whiskey' for a cold or brandy for a shock is usually not advised. There are alternative ways of dealing with both.
- Teenagers will notice not just the amount you drink but why you drink, when you drink, and the effects of drink on you. They will also notice if you drink when alone, drink when there is a problem, drink without food, or drink at the end of the day. Remember that they are observing your behaviour, and take appropriate care.
- Encourage self-esteem, be positive about your teenagers, and help them develop self-confidence. Studies show that those who abuse alcohol often have problems with self-esteem and are less resistant to the need to drink.
- Encourage participation in sport and other social activities.
- Help your child to overcome any problems with shyness, because people with 'social phobia' often turn to alcohol as a social lubricant.
- From a young age, stress that people who achieve things in life often don't drink or drink very moderately.
- Tuning in early to their problems at school or with friends, and showing you care, will diminish the risk of your adolescent turning to drink.
- Don't have alcohol too visible or too easily accessible.
- If adolescents come in drunk, be kind and careful about their health and safety that night, and wait until the follow-

ing day to discuss it. Above all, try not to react with emotion.

- Try not to say things like, 'I could murder a pint', 'I'm dying for a drink', 'I'll just have one for the road', 'He's a great drinker,' or 'He can hold his drink'. They give the wrong message to the adolescent.
- If a parent has a problem with drink, don't deny it. Denial is dangerous, because it is such an integral part of alcoholism. Instead, explain the problem that the parent has, using it as an example of the power of alcohol.
- Don't wait for the problem to go away; it never does.
- If your adolescent has a problem with drink, get professional help, both for the problem and for the factors which caused it in the first place.

There is a temptation not to confront the problem of teenage drinking. There is also uncertainty about whether to sit down and explain the use and abuse of alcohol. Indeed, there are doubts as to whether the explanations provided may encourage a teenager to drink, therefore having an effect opposite to that which was intended.

However, it is important to provide clear, unambiguous information about the responsible use of alcohol and the dangers caused by alcohol abuse. It is best that this information be provided by you at an early stage in the adolescent's development.

DRUG ABUSE

MANY TEENAGERS SAY THAT ADULTS have double standards about drugs. They object to adults lecturing them on the topic of drugs, arguing that the adult population uses cigarettes, alcohol, tranquillisers, excessive caffeine (in tea, coffee) and sleeping pills. They express disregard for the adult who, with an alcoholic drink in one hand and a cigarette in the other, warns them of the dangers of drug abuse.

Adolescents also notice if popping pills is used as a quick response to pain within their family. This influences their attitude towards drugs in general and their acceptance of personal drug-taking in particular. It is not surprising, therefore, that the distinction between legal and illegal drug-taking is one which sometimes escapes them.

Certainly amongst adolescents, it is impossible to know the extent of the drug abuse problem because of the illegal and hidden nature of much adolescent use. Also, the relative popularity of illegal drugs changes rapidly as new drugs appear on the adolescent 'scene' or as familiar substances (glue, aerosols) become misused.

In addition, 'Ecstasy', or MDMA (methylenedioxymethamphetamine), which has a vast number of street names, such as 'Shamrocks', 'Adam', 'Disco Biscuits', 'E', 'XTC', 'Doves', arrived in Ireland only in the early 1990s. Relatives of MDMA, known as 'Eve' and 'MDA', are also prevalent. Furthermore, the arrival of new substances and the range of names by which they are commonly known, adds to the confusion in identifying the degree of usage.

At the time of writing, there have been 20 reported deaths from Ecstasy in Ireland. It has also been reported that more than 2,000 people a year avail of the drug treatment services in

Dublin. Cork and Limerick are reported to have even higher rates of illegal drug use than Dublin.

In one survey of Irish school children, 13% were reported to have abused solvents at some stage in their school life. Furthermore, 4% of Irish school children have taken 'magic mushrooms', and 13% of Dublin adolescents reported using cannabis at some stage. The extent of Ecstasy use is unknown, but is regarded as exceptionally high. The use of heroin is reportedly rising.

It is estimated that about 20% of young people may try some form of substance taking. Figures suggest that about 2% will take hard drugs, but statistics may be very inaccurate with regard to illegal usage.

However, even without conclusive statistics, we can still be sure that our adolescents are likely to be offered drugs. They are also likely to be in the presence of other adolescents who use drugs, and they may themselves, at some stage, try one or more of the widely available range of drugs marketed for teenage use.

WHY DO TEENAGERS USE DRUGS?

There are many classic reasons why adolescents will try some form of illegal substance:

- As an escape from reality, to help cope with worries, with loneliness or depression.
- As an attempt to gain some status, particularly if self-esteem is low.
- As a rite of passage, or because of a need to be part of a group.
- The excitement of trying something that is forbidden.
- Experimentation and risk-taking, as a part of growing up.
- Being influenced by friends, and finding it difficult to say 'no'.

93

- Being a target for drug-pushers, and falling for their inducements.
- As an expression of upset or revenge directed at parents or those in authority (teachers or police).
- Out of simple curiosity, boredom, or having nothing else to do.
- Because of the pleasurable experience of drug consumption, or because a dependence is formed.

WHAT SHOULD PARENTS LOOK OUT FOR?

Almost anything can signal drug abuse, but it is the pattern of usage which is important in deciding if your adolescent is involved in drug misuse.

Irish studies show that adolescents may take a variety of drugs, making it more difficult to distinguish what has been taken. Furthermore, because illegally purchased drugs are sometimes adulterated, the effects on the adolescent can depend on what other substance the drug has been diluted with or 'cut' with. Sadly, in Ireland, there have been some cases where adulteration has resulted in death.

Unfortunately, for some parents, their first knowledge of their adolescent's substance abuse has come through a phone call from a hospital, describing how their child is suffering a harmful reaction, an overdose, or an accident or injury brought about under the influence of the drug.

Alternatively, many parents discover that their child has misused drugs only when informed by the school that they are part of a group caught taking, or selling, an illegal substance. Being aware of the likely signs may protect you from hearing that your adolescent has misused drugs in these distressing ways.

The following indicators of adolescent drug abuse may be helpful:

- Sudden and unexpected mood or personality changes.
- Odd or unusual marks, or stains on clothes.
- Unidentifiable or unusual body odour from the adolescent.
- Aggressive and challenging behaviour at home or at school.
- Shutting themselves in their bedroom, having returned from being out with friends.
- Leaving scorched tinfoil in pockets or in the bedroom.
- Being secretive about their whereabouts or vague about activities.
- Staying out excessively late at night, contrary to their parents' wishes.
- Exhibiting euphoria, elation, inappropriate laughing or strange reactions, particularly having just returned home.
- Appearing physically depressed or excessively active on return from a disco, particularly a 'rave' disco.
- Poor concentration, forgetfulness, poor attention, or poor comprehension.
- Tiredness, restlessness, or lack of energy.
- Change in friendships, particularly if new friends appear 'strange' or reluctant to come into the home.
- Excessive demands for money.
- Grinding of teeth, or licking lips excessively.
- Dizziness, slurring of speech.
- Solvents disappearing from the home. (It is advisable to keep track of your purchase of these.)
- Excessive use of hairspray, deodorants, requests for room fresheners (which may be used for the wrong purpose).
- Unusual powders or tablets in the adolescent's possession.
- Telling lies, and showing great anger or upset when found out.
- Phone calls or visits from 'friends' that seem to make the adolescent upset or fearful.
- Sudden decline in schoolwork.

- Inability to get up for school in the morning, and the appearance of being hung-over.
- Smell of a solvent on the breath, or a red ring around the mouth and nose (which is known as 'glue sniffer's rash').
- Traces of solvent on sleeves, on handkerchiefs, in bottles, or in crisp packets or plastic bags.
- Unexplained burns or rashes.
- Change in appetite, especially unusual loss of appetite or desperate hunger.
- Feelings of nausea.
- Unexplained disappearance of money from the house.

WHAT DRUGS COULD MY TEENAGER BE TAKING?

There are three reasons why it is not easy to know if your teenager is using drugs and what drugs they may be taking. Firstly, the signs of use can depend on the type of drug being abused. Secondly, some of the signs of drug misuse can mimic other adolescent moods and behaviours. Thirdly, some drugs can cause a confusing range of effects.

Drugs can be broadly categorised under the following headings: hallucinogens, volatile solvents, stimulants, opiates, and sedatives. The following guidelines to the drugs and their effects may be helpful:

Hallucinogens. These can range from LSD to solvents and magic mushrooms, and can cause confusion, distortion of reality, hallucinations, and feelings of paranoia. It is worth noting that one Dublin survey of schoolchildren showed that 4% had taken 'magic mushrooms'.

Volatile Solvents. Volatile Substance Abuse is the technical term used to describe a range of behaviours with substances, with the inhalation of many gases, chemical fumes or vapours. Solvents are chemicals which change into gases or vapours. Household products such as hair lacquer, glues, lighter fuel, nail varnish remover, paint stripper, insect sprays, correction fluids, room deodorants and petrol, contain a range of different chemical solvents. The term 'glue sniffing' is inaccurate because many products other than 'glue' are involved, and also because many of the products are taken directly into the mouth.

Volatile solvents may be categorised as hallucinogens because an hallucinogenic effect can occur, but they really deserve to be categorised separately because of the very widespread use of solvents by young people.

Solvent abuse is primarily an activity of the young adolescent. As many as 13% of Dublin adolescents have reported experimenting with solvents and, interestingly, the use of solvents outside of Dublin is estimated to be even higher. Additionally, solvent abuse is greater amongst boys than girls.

Stimulants. These range from nicotine and caffeine to cocaine and amphetamines (which are synthetic stimulants). They can cause physical and mental hyperactivity, depending on the mood of the person using them and on how much of the drug is being taken. Ecstasy is a stimulant, and has properties of both amphetamines and hallucinogens.

When other amphetamines, such as 'speed', 'ice', 'crystal', 'purple hearts', 'uppers', 'whizz' are discontinued, depression, hunger and sleepiness can result. Regular users can display aggressive or violent behaviour and hostility if they develop the psychosis which is associated with their abuse.

Cocaine is a stimulant which rapidly brings about feelings of euphoria. It is also referred to as 'snow', 'crack' or 'coke'. It is identified as a drug that brings about psychological dependence because of its particularly pleasurable effects. It is usually sniffed (snorting) as a powder, but can be injected. Sometimes it is heated (in tinfoil) and the vapours inhaled. This is called 'chasing the dragon.' Symptoms of use include restlessness, anxiousness, or suspiciousness.

Opiates. These include heroin ('smack', 'skag'), morphine, codeine, or synthetically-made drugs which tend to cause drowsiness and a slowing-down of physical activity, and the user can seem to be detached from reality. There has been a steady increase in the use of heroin in this country, despite the fact that the daily cost of addiction can run into hundreds of pounds.

Sedatives. These include alcohol, tranquillisers, sleeping tablets, and can cause poor coordination, staggering, or slurring of speech. The illegal use of barbiturates ('downers', 'barbs') has reportedly fallen in this country, perhaps being replaced by a new range of substances on the market.

Cannabis ('dope', 'blow', 'grass', 'weed') is one of the most widely used illegal drugs. It has both sedative and hallucinogenic elements. It also has different names, depending on what part of the plant is used. Marijuana comes from the leaves. Hashish comes from the resin of the plant and is usually smoked in 'joints', which are home-made cigarettes containing the substance. Hashish Oil, which is one of the most popular forms of cannabis in Ireland, is a concentrated extract.

The effects of cannabis are most noticeable in schoolwork because of memory impairment, the reduction in learning ability, mood swings, and poor judgement that follow from its use. One survey of Dublin adolescents showed that 13% had used cannabis at least once.

Cannabis is widely perceived by teenagers as a harmless drug, with mostly positive effects for the user. Research, however, indicates many adverse effects, including psychological addiction, the development of tolerance, symptoms of withdrawal following long-term use, and evidence that the drug has cancer-causing properties.

WHAT CAN A PARENT DO?

As parents, we can begin by being well-informed about drugs and by arming ourselves with information about the effects of different drugs on the market.

Often, adolescents, while being very well-versed in how to use drugs, have little clear knowledge about the dangerous effects. Adolescence is a time when one feels indestructible, and many do not take warnings seriously, particularly if we do not communicate honestly about the relative dangers of the various substances.

In addition, parents play a very important role in helping adolescents to resist drugs in the following ways:

- Adhering to a strict model of behaviour in their use of substances. Alcohol consumption that is moderate, and behaviour surrounding alcohol that is safe, such as not drinking and driving, is a most powerful example to young people.

- Not smoking, thereby sending adolescents a message about respect for one's health and the health of those you live with. If you do smoke, admitting that this is a harmful addiction is better than arguing that smoking is not illegal. Express regret that you began smoking, and explain to the adolescent that it is hard to free yourself from the grip of the drug.

- Take care with the family's use of painkillers and other tablets from a young age. This helps to develop a healthy respect for, and awareness of, the potency of drugs.

- Cultivate and nurture your relationship with your adolescent child. An adolescent who is happy at home and can communicate with parents, is much less likely to need the escapism of drug use.

- Do your utmost to develop the self-esteem of the adolescent, as discussed in other chapters. This is one of the most powerful protectors from all the dangers that beset adolescents, including the likelihood of drug misuse.

- Always know where your child is, and who they are with.
- Leave newspaper articles highlighting the dangers of drug abuse where the adolescent will see them.
- If there is a particularly good television programme on drug abuse, record it for them and invite them to watch it for themselves, if they wish.
- Explain that you are really concerned about the health risks of drug abuse. Be honest in your description of the risks, and don't describe all drug abuse as if it involved mainlining heroin with infected needles.
- Express your contempt for those who make a fortune by exploiting adolescents, especially drug-pushers. Ensure adolescents know that, far from being independent, they are pawns of the corrupt and greedy in our society.
- Express your concern for those parents whose children may be taking drugs, and talk about how lucky you are to have such a mature and sensible adolescent. Adolescents are very good at living up to our expectations of them.

WHAT CAN A TEACHER DO?

- Watch out for constant lateness amongst pupils, particularly if they are moody or irritable on arrival at school. Something is likely to be wrong if the student's pattern of behaviour changes.
- Be alert to a sudden and sustained deterioration in school performance.
- Be aware of any lack of attention in class in a student who was previously attentive.
- Watch our for small groups of students congregating in corridors, cloakrooms, bike-sheds.

- Be sensitive to any restlessness, irritability, or aggression in a student who was previously manageable and compliant.
- Note the absence of any abusable products from the science laboratory, the workroom, or the school office.
- Be vigilant for any increase in truancy or absenteeism. Notify parents of any change in a pupil's behaviour pattern.

HOW SHOULD I REACT IF I FIND MY ADOLESCENT IS TAKING DRUGS?
If you do find that your teenager is experimenting with drugs, get professional help immediately. Don't reassure yourself that this is the first time; it may simply be the first time they were found out.

- Medical or psychiatric evaluation is important in situations of long-term abuse or if the adolescent finds it difficult to abstain.
- Try to understand and address why your adolescent got involved in the first place. When young people have misused substances, try to talk to them gently about the worries they have. Try to imagine what may have caused them to misuse drugs. Do not be afraid to get help from professionals, and do not be afraid to discuss any family worries, difficulties or concerns with them.
- If you find an adolescent under the influence of a drug, do *not* get angry or panic. A sudden reaction could be harmful while they are still under the drug's influence. It would be particularly dangerous, from a medical point of view, to chase away or become aggressive with an adolescent group if you surprise them in the course of abusing solvents.
- Collect samples of the substance your adolescent is abusing for the purpose of analysis. You need to know exactly what your adolescent has taken and its likely effects. The analysis is also for health reasons, in case any other harmful agents may have been mixed with it. Explain this to the

adolescent, to show your concern for their health.

While there is no doubt that drugs are freely available, many young people are well able to resist them. Others will experiment and make mistakes, which can be an opportunity for learning rather than a catastrophe. Knowing about drugs, and knowing how to handle the situation should you discover drug taking by your adolescent, is important.

It is not the end of the world if you find that your adolescent has experimented with drugs. Instead, it is a time requiring consideration, help and support, thereby ensuring that they are safe from any future recurrence. It may also be a time to help them with other worries, which may have caused the drug taking in the first instance.

SEPARATION AND DIVORCE

MANY PARENTS MAY VIEW SEPARATION and divorce as a solution to their problems. However, these events are usually experienced by their children as upsetting, distressing or depressing, and in many cases cause a total disruption to their lives.

At a conservative estimate, there are many tens of thousands of Irish children who have gone through the process of family separation. Many more are facing the imminence of family breakup. The emotional consequences that are involved require our careful consideration.

The fact that divorcing families and, in particular, the children in these families, represent a significant and growing population whose needs require examination and understanding, is widely recognised. There have been many substantial investigations of the problem, most notably in America, where the work of Wallerstein and Kelly since the 1970s has extensively examined the problems involved.

Their conclusions regarding the difficulties that arise for young people are supported by further research and clinical studies in the Irish context. The following is an examination of the multiplicity of factors which have been identified to date and which ought to be understood if the problems arising from separation are to be properly tackled.

ADOLESCENT RESPONSES TO SEPARATION AND DIVORCE

For adolescents, family breakup has been described as an experience of 'unparalleled stress and psychological pain'. Reactions may include feelings of shock, fear, self-blame, anger, sadness and grieving. Additionally, adolescents may encounter problems in their emotional development, in their relationships with parents, in sexual development, and in academic achievement. We will examine each of these under their separate headings.

EMOTIONAL DEVELOPMENT

In order to deal with the multiple losses occasioned by family breakup, adolescents use particular strategies to cope emotionally. These strategies include the following:

- Distancing themselves from the pain by keeping busy, denying that the breakup has any emotional effect on them, and using humour and sarcasm to mask the problems.
- Reacting with acute sadness, anguish, grief and mourning, at a time when they are already experiencing the traumatic loss of childhood.
- Experiencing feelings of being 'caught in the middle', with conflicting loyalties to both parents.
- Experiencing loneliness for the parent who has left, particularly if a good and growing relationship existed beforehand.
- Experiencing upset if a parent has left to live with another person.
- Worrying about the future, the scarcity of money, and the possible danger that they will not have sufficient resources to buy clothes or other symbols of adolescent prestige.
- Worrying that their academic aspirations may not be realisable due to lack of finance.
- Constantly looking for targets of blame for the separation or divorce.
- Feeling excessive concern for the health and welfare of the parent who remains at home, and being fearful about the death of this remaining source of support.

RELATIONSHIP WITH PARENTS

- Experiencing resentment and anger at being called upon to be involved in parental disputes.
- Feeling distraught now that their view of their parents as stable, trustworthy and reliable has been challenged.
- Having to come to terms with a changed relationship with parents, especially difficult at a time when they are already negotiating similar changes as part of the normal adolescent process.
- Being confronted with ambivalent rules regarding discipline, and the possibility that each of the separated parents will impose different rules.
- Having no 'court of appeal', now that one-half of the parental authority is gone.
- Punishing the parents for their action by aggressive and challenging behaviour.
- Obstructing attempts by the separated parents to establish new sexual relationships.
- Rejecting parents as role models, because they no longer meet the previous idealised standards.
- Being embarrassed about their parents' more visible sexuality, now that the parents are 'single' people again.

SEXUAL DEVELOPMENT

- Becoming concerned about their own future ability to enter into enduring relationships.
- Becoming disillusioned and cynical about romance and marriage.
- Engaging in inappropriate and early sexual activity as a means of expressing confusion or anger towards parents.
- Rejecting normal opposite-sex encounters, and becoming distrustful or disillusioned about the sincerity of enduring relationships with others.

105

- Experiencing sexual confusion regarding their attitudes to the parents' new sexual partners, e.g., a daughter's view of a new stepfather.
- Fearing that the new partner may cross sexual boundaries, and behave in an inappropriate sexual manner towards the teenagers.

ACADEMIC ACHIEVEMENT

Research shows that academic progress may be disrupted for one to two years after separation, and even more time may have been lost in the build-up to separation. The following are some of the difficulties involved:

- Finding it hard to concentrate at school, which is especially difficult when sitting examinations such as the Junior Certificate or Leaving Certificate.
- Receiving less support and encouragement from the parents than before.
- Receiving less help with homework from their parents than in the past, thereby feeling alone in their academic endeavours.
- Being put under extreme academic pressure by parents who wish to allay their own feelings of guilt and prove that the separation has not negatively affected their children.
- Having genuine learning disorders, such as written language disorders or specific maths problems, attributed to the separation and divorce when, in fact, they require independent assessment and treatment.
- Engaging in elaborate deceptions at school to hide their family status from teachers and friends.
- No longer inviting school-friends to their home, for fear that the absence of a parent will be recognised.
- Avoiding sporting activities or events to which both par-

ents have been invited.

- Experiencing particular sadness and yearning at the critical points in academic life, such as the celebration of Junior Certificate or Leaving Certificate success, the deb's ball, school plays, or successful accession to Third Level education. Such events can reaffirm the teenager's different status and can initiate a recurrence of grief and mourning which the adolescent thought they had resolved.

DIFFERENCES BETWEEN BOYS AND GIRLS

Because it is more usual for fathers to leave the family home, the experience of separation has been found to be different for boys and girls in the following ways:

Adolescence is a time when boys and girls seek identification with the same-sex parent as part of the process of moving into their adult roles. Studies also show that adolescent adjustment is linked to the quality of the relationship with the same-sex parent. Therefore, the departure of the father from the family home removes the continuity of this identification process for boys, disrupting this important developmental process.

However, studies also show that a good quality relationship with fathers, after parental separation, is important for good self-esteem and the absence of depression in *both* girls and boys.

When the breakup has been acrimonious, particularly if the mother feels angry and betrayed by the father, this may lead to adolescent boys receiving negative messages about males. The previously positive goal of 'being like dad' may become a fear of being 'just like your father'. In this way, boys may withdraw from identification with fathers, so as not to threaten the relationship with their mothers.

Furthermore, research has shown that when mothers perceive their sons as similar to their ex-spouse, they may direct negative feelings towards them. This can leave boys feeling rejected, particularly if they reside in all-female households.

Equally, there is a danger that fathers may displace their anger towards their ex-spouse onto the daughter. This may have the effect of lowering the daughter's self-esteem and making her fear that she is 'unlovable'. However, because young girls usually live with their mothers, the impact is often reduced.

Because some fathers believe that time spent with their sons is important, they may spend more time with them than with their daughters. Likewise, some fathers may be more confident in their relationships with their sons and less certain in their relationships with their daughters. This could have the effect of encouraging adolescent girls to interpret their gender negatively.

Research shows that adolescent boys may resent being left behind by their fathers when they leave the family home. In a situation where a mother feels negatively about males, then the boys can feel doubly abandoned.

Boys in all-female households are often cast in the role of 'man-of-the-house', and are given responsibility for heavy tasks including putting out the bins and lifting buckets of coal. Girls may find themselves being given more traditional female tasks, such as cooking and cleaning and minding younger siblings. This may cause resentment, in some cases.

Theories of attachment show that normal emotional development depends on secure emotional attachments in early life. Because of disharmony and the difficulties of family break-up, the loss of a parent through separation and divorce has been found to carry an even greater emotional risk than loss through death.

Finally, depressive illness is much more common in boys who have lost their fathers, although both boys and girls are at risk of depression in the post-separation period. Likewise, both boys and girls express uncertainty about their capacity to love and to be loved in the future, and many fear marriage or see the future demise of their own marriages as inevitable.

HOW YOU CAN HELP
Emotional needs

- Acknowledge that adolescents have the right to grieve the loss of the family, and allow the grieving process to take place. (Many parents feel guilty about separation and therefore may discourage the expression of distress in their children, finding it too painful to witness.)
- Allow the adolescent to talk about their sense of loss for the parent who has left. (This is very important for the happiness and emotional development of the adolescent, and will attach them even more warmly to you.)
- Emphasise to the adolescent that it is the parents that are separating from each other, and that they are not separating from their children. (Tell them that both of you will continue to be their parents. The emotional development of the young person depends on the continuation of the parenting role.)
- Do not seek emotional support from your adolescent son or daughter. (This is an overwhelming burden for many adolescents, who themselves are likely to be in need of emotional support.)
- Try not to involve your adolescent if you are not coping. (If you are suffering emotionally and unable to cope, seek professional help for yourself.)
- Try not to take your anxiety and moods out on your adolescent.
- Try not to embarrass the adolescent by leaving any school bills unpaid because your ex-spouse has not provided the

money.

- Don't involve the teenager when establishing financial agreements with your ex-spouse, and don't demand over-due money in their presence.

Financial concerns
- Protect the adolescent from any financial difficulties the breakup may have imposed on you. (If your financial circumstances have disimproved, be honest and sympathetic towards your teenagers about luxuries you can no longer afford, but reassure them about the basics of food, shelter and education.)
- If the adolescent asks for money you don't have, do not say, 'Ask your father' or 'Ask your mother'. (Parents need to work out financial arrangements in advance.)
- Do not be angry if you are asked for money that you cannot afford. (It takes time for adolescents to adjust to an altered economic lifestyle.)
- Ensure, if possible, that your child can afford school outings or other school activities, so that they do not feel excluded.
- If you must say 'no' to requests because money is tight, be sympathetic but firm in your response.
- Never 'throw' money at your children to compensate for the problems they are experiencing due to the family break-up.
- Parents should not compete with each other by lavishing money and gifts on the child.

Attitude towards the absent parent
- Try not to speak negatively about the absent parent, regardless of the anger, injustice or upset you may feel.
- Never seek alliances with adolescents against the other

parent. (If you seek alliances you may find it difficult to impose discipline.)

- Be aware that conflicts of loyalty can be overwhelming for adolescents. (Understand that adolescents may lie to each parent about their view of the other.)
- Except in cases of child abuse or violence, you should try to foster contacts between the adolescent and the absent spouse. (Phone calls, calling to the home, or spending extra time with the other parent will help to strengthen the adolescent's sense of having two parents who care and are available.)
- Do all you can to encourage the absent parent to be supportive to the young person. (If the absent parent is unreliable, inattentive, or not available, try to help the adolescent to cope with their disappointment, sense of rejection or betrayal. Do not add to their hurt by suggesting that the other parent 'doesn't want you' or 'doesn't care'.)
- If the teenager's relationship with the absent parent was one in which the young person felt frightened, threatened or anxious, do not insist that they visit, and arrange for a psychological or psychiatric investigation to determine your child's best interests.

Access arrangements
- It is advised not to use legal terms such as 'access' when discussing visiting arrangements. The term 'spending time with' is more positive and less threatening.
- Carefully consider the pros and cons of 'joint custody', in which the child lives equally in the homes of both parents. Consider the practicality of having two bedrooms, two sets of clothes, books and treasured possessions. Ask yourself if your child's best interests are served by dividing their time between two locations?

- If you are the parent who is away from home, try to be reliable, consistent and punctual when visits have been arranged. (Studies show that intense pain, anger, frustration, disappointment and rejection are experienced by adolescents when a parent lets them down. Cancelling arrangements, unless absolutely necessary, sends a message to adolescents that other activities in your life are more important to you than they are.)
- Never obstruct access as a tactic to force the absent parent to pay maintenance. (Non-payment of maintenance can be dealt with legally, if necessary.)
- Never cancel visiting rights as a form of punishment for the other parent. (Genuine grievances should be dealt with by other means. When access is used as a weapon by either parent, young people suffer enormously.)
- Allow the adolescent some flexibility in access arrangements. (A rigid schedule can be difficult for adolescents who are developing their own interests and activities during their free time. Adolescents have the right to be consulted about access times, and they can be resentful if those times are decided for them.)
- If there is more than one child involved, do not insist that access always be undertaken together. (Different children, and especially children of differing ages, have different developmental needs and interests. As a result, individual time with children of different ages and gender may be advisable.)
- Do not ask teenagers to carry messages to the other parent. (In particular, adolescents resent being asked to request money from the other parent.)
- Resist using adolescents as 'informers' about the life or activities of the other parent. (Adolescents hate being asked for details about the other parent's life, particularly if such

information might be used as 'ammunition' against that parent in legal proceedings.)

- If you are the absent parent, try to provide a pleasant apartment or home to which you can bring your children. (Days spent in frantic entertainment may not allow normal time to relate to your adolescent.)
- Be sensitive to the fact that adolescents will not always be good-humoured or cheerful on return from access visits. (Adolescents may feel sad, angry or confused after access, and may behave badly. Interpret this for what it is: a symptom of their emotions.)
- Be aware that many adolescents behave much better with the 'absent' parent than with the 'custodial' or primary minder. (Clinical experience suggests that this is because they may be afraid that the parent who left will abandon them altogether if their behaviour is challenging or non-compliant. Both parents need to be aware of this insecurity and should reassure the adolescent that they will never abandon their role as a concerned parent.)

Meeting a new partner

- Understand that adolescents will resent sharing their access time with a new person in your life. (If you are a parent who has left home, do not expect adolescents to be as delighted as you are with your new relationship. Do not interpret their resentment as a sign that the adolescent is taking sides. Understand that adolescents, particularly initially, will be jealous of anyone who dilutes your time with them.)
- Try not to behave as an 'adolescent' in your enthusiasm for your new relationship. (Adolescents need a parent, not another 'adolescent', to guide them.)
- Be sensitive to sleeping arrangements when children have

overnight access. (In two-parent families, parents' sexuality is hidden and discrete and most adolescents prefer to think of their parents as sexually dormant. The increased visibility of parents' sexual interests may be unsettling to adolescents who are struggling with their own sexual identity.)

- If parents are engaged in new relationships, it is advisable to keep these at as great a distance as possible until children have adapted to the distress of the family breakup.
- Do not expose adolescents to a *series* of new relationships. Remember that you cannot expect your adolescent to behave in a sexually responsible fashion if they believe their parents to be acting differently.

WHAT CAN TEACHERS DO?

Adolescents whose parents are separating, or have separated, may face difficulties with academic progress and emotional stability in school. The following guidelines may be helpful for teachers:

- Be sensitive to the stresses adolescents may be under. Making some allowances for less compliant, irritable or frustrated behaviour can be useful.
- Expect a possible deterioration in school performance, but try to encourage the adolescent not to lose too much ground during this time.
- School counsellors are an important resource for adolescents who wish to discuss their upset. However, adolescents may resent being automatically sent to the counsellor because their parents have separated.
- Don't assume that all families are two-parent families when requesting information about home, when assigning essays, or when seeking parents' signatures.
- Don't make negative comments about 'broken homes'.

- Restrict classroom discussions about separation to the 'facts', and include some compassion and sympathy for the families that have experienced separation or divorce.
- Remember that some adolescents will produce extremely disruptive behaviour in school in an effort to test their parents' response or to show their parents that they are upset. They may be covertly forcing both parents to unite in response to the problem.
- Be careful not to automatically interpret an adolescent's poor behaviour or school problems as exclusively emanating from the family breakup. Other conditions might apply, such as a learning problem or experimentation with alcohol or drugs. These require attention in their own right.
- Be aware of the new financial constraints the adolescent's family may be experiencing when requesting contributions for additional school materials, special events, or school outings.
- Examine your own views and prejudices about family breakup, and ensure that they do not make their way into the classroom.

At the end of the day, studies show that most young people wish to live in a two-parent family. Because of that, separation and divorce can be traumatic during the teenage years, imposing a wide range of additional burdens on teenagers.

How adolescents cope with family breakup depends on how the multiple difficulties surrounding it are attended to. Ensuring that decisions are made in the best interests of young people will do a lot to overcome the acute grief, loss, disruption and dangers associated with separation and divorce.

BEREAVEMENT

TOO OFTEN IT IS ASSUMED that, because teenagers are young, they don't have a viewpoint or an appreciation of the death of another. In fact, studies show that entirely the opposite is the case. The loss of a person who is an integral part of the adolescent's world, particularly if this is a family member, is an acute, profound and painful loss experienced at the deepest level of the adolescent's being.

We think of adolescence as a time when life is most lived and when death seems most distant, as a time of vitality, energy, risk, passion, and belief in immortality. This belief in immortality is shattered by the adolescent's first encounter with death.

The adolescent's first experience of death could follow from the loss of anyone close to them, including the passing away of a parent, a grandparent, a brother or sister, a friend, or a teacher who doesn't return to school. The effects on the teenager may even follow from the death of a family pet.

Suddenly, the adolescent faces the concept of their own death, and this challenges many of the certainties that existed in their lives. It also challenges the permanence of existing structures, the permanence of parents, of life, of self, and of security and safety. All of these losses happen at a time when adolescents are already confused; a time of great vulnerability when they are seeking stability and security.

STAGES OF GRIEVING

The worst time for many families is when the funeral is over and the shock and numbness have worn off. This is normally followed by great sadness, loneliness, and the full impact of the loss. At this stage, the family will begin their individual and collective journeys through the process of grief, which will extend over the weeks and months ahead.

While grief has recognised and documented stages, it is also a very personal experience and is bound up with the particular relationship the adolescent had with the person who died. Research has identified the phases and stages, emotions and reactions of the grieving process, along with the myriad experiences a person may encounter when faced with the death of another:

Shock – This is usually the first reaction to the news of a death, and the numbness is nature's shield from the impact of the news.

Denial – Phrases such as, 'I can't believe he's dead', or 'I just can't take it in', spring from the difficulty we all have in encompassing death's finality.

Searching – This involves intense and overwhelming sadness, restlessness, pining, uncontrollable yearning, and 'searching' for the person who is gone.

Despair – Despair can set in with the realisation that no amount of searching or yearning will recover the dead person.

Anger – Anger towards the person who has departed is a common experience in grief. The adolescent wonders, 'Why did you have to die?' or 'How could you leave me now?'

Anxiety – If a parent has died, adolescents may worry about the health of the other parent, about their aspirations for college being no longer financially possible, about their new responsibilities in the family, and about their ability to cope.

Guilt – There are always feelings of guilt and thoughts of 'if only', when someone dies. These feelings overlap with all the other stages of grieving and are particularly painful for adolescents. This is so because they may have been in a normal conflictual relationship with their parents and, in

117

the event of a parent dying, they are now cut off from re-
solving the conflict.

These stages should not be regarded as an inevitable pattern.
Nor is it necessary to go through the stages in sequence or even
to experience all of them. Each stage will affect the adolescent,
and the process may also be accompanied by the following
generalised symptoms of distress:

- Alarming mood swings, ranging from tears to hysterical
  laughter.
- Fears of rejection, abandonment, desertion, and great fears
  of change.
- Feelings of emptiness, shame, betrayal, being unlovable,
  being incomplete.
- A deep sense of loss, and of being denied time with the
  person who died.
- Attempts to dampen and stifle emotions, in order to mini-
  mise hurt.
- Fantasies, idealisation, and 'halo' effects, which interfere
  with accurate memories.
- Blaming the person who died, by asking questions such as,
  'Why did you smoke?', 'Why weren't you careful?'
- Psychosomatic illnesses, or symptoms that may mimic the
  cause of death, such as chest pains, choking sensations,
  feeling faint.
- Sleeplessness, dreams, nightmares, a change in sleeping
  patterns, and awakening unrefreshed.
- Feelings of depression, tearfulness, apathy, irritability, help-
  lessness, and hopelessness.
- Wanting to be with others, wanting to be alone, needing
  friends and yet rejecting them at the same time.
- Dreading school, being unable to concentrate, being dis-

organised, anxious, forgetful about homework, and wondering what is the point of it all?
- Regret for the past, and fearfulness for the future.
- Feelings of being overwhelmed by the physical pain and the strength of emotions.
- Dreading the process of sorting out possessions, of destroying the last vestiges of the dead person's physical presence.
- Painful memories evoked by a tune, a smell, the texture of a jacket, or a familiar programme on television.

DEATH OF A PARENT

The death of a parent during the adolescent years is a deep and untimely loss. This loss shatters the adolescent's core of security, sense of protection, sense of identity, source of love, and sense of certainty about the future.

While a parent grieves deeply for the loss of their partner of many years, the adolescent grieves for someone they have known *all their lives*. The parent will not see them as an adult, will not know their successes, will not be grandparent to their children.

If the relationship was warm, the adolescent may remember the parent teaching them to swim, bringing them to football matches or to dancing classes, to birthday parties, on trips to the zoo. They may also recollect cut knees being bandaged, the first bike, the picnics, the walks, being carried home.

When a mother dies, there are many physical memories of being held, being fed, the fragrance of the mother, and her softness and gentleness to the child. When a father dies, there are many memories of the security, the strength, the fun, being thrown in the air, playing in the garden, or being given a pocketful of sweets.

Worse still, the death is likely to have happened at a time

when adolescents are moving away from the parents, trying to become individual and separate, and now finding themselves separated forever.

The inevitable conflicts, mistakes, challenges, rudeness, bad behaviour, anger, which are normal at this stage, can haunt the adolescent and generate feelings of guilt. During the worst pangs of guilt, the adolescent can feel responsible for the parent's death, for causing them stress, making them ill.

Consider the following as short-term and longer-term guides to understanding and helping the adolescent through this time:

In the short-term
- Make sure, if you are the surviving parent, that *you* tell them the news of the death, especially if the death is sudden and unexpected. You are the next source of their love and security.
- Give them the facts, such as, 'It was a heart attack', or 'There was no pain'.
- *Don't* say, 'Be brave', 'Have courage', 'Don't cry', 'Don't be sad'. Grief is about feeling pain; sadness is necessary, bravery is repression.
- Don't be upset if they react angrily, remain silent and un-comprehending, laugh, break down, walk out, or scream. There is no 'right' response to death.
- Try not to burden the adolescent by saying, 'You're the man of the house now', or 'You are now the mother to your sisters'. They are adolescents, not parents.
- Console them if they feel responsible for the death, or if they fought with the parent the last time they saw them.
- Console them if you know that the parent had said something hurtful to the adolescent before the death, particularly something like, 'You're a disgrace', or 'You'll be the

death of me'.

- Invite them to tell their friends, or invite a close friend to the house. Friends are very important to young people at this time.
- Keep them active and involved, by asking them to help in informing relations of the death. The process of relaying the news can be therapeutic.
- Where a parent dies after a prolonged illness, console the adolescent who was present at the death, no matter how lingering and gentle it was. You may use phrases such as, 'We got to say goodbye', 'In time, you will be glad you were there', 'She saw how much you loved her', or 'He was glad we were with him when he died'.
- Console the adolescent who was not there for the final demise and may feel cheated, particularly if the hospital visits had been on a daily basis. Use phrases such as, 'He must have chosen it this way, so as not to upset you', or 'She preferred to go quietly in the end'.
- Confirm your continuing love and support as much as you can, by saying, 'I'm here to help you', 'I'll always stick by you', or 'Don't forget I'm around'.
- Give the adolescent a special possession belonging to the parent as a memento. Consider something that they might also pass on to their children, such as a watch, a ring, a favourite book.
- Invite the adolescent to help with the funeral arrangements; choosing the flowers, selecting or delivering one of the readings, writing a personal message on a bouquet of flowers.
- Talk to the adolescent about viewing the body. Some people prefer to remember the person when they were vibrant and alive and to retain those memories unaltered by the heavy, cold, marble-stillness of death. An adolescent should never

be forced to see or kiss a body.

- Occupy the young person after the funeral by serving drinks, making tea, looking after relations. Be sure to invite some of their friends back to the house.

In the longer-term

Once the immediate days have passed, and the funeral and burial are over, the adolescent will continue to have many needs and requirements in coping with their grief. Their emotional problems during this time may persist, and you might help them in the following ways:

- Never assume that because an adolescent is not showing their grief in the conventional manner, than they are not grieving at all.
- Allow, invite, but do not demand discussion of death. While providing an opportunity to talk about feelings is important, adolescents often find it difficult to articulate their feelings and may be stressed if called upon to do so.
- Do not be afraid to show your own grief as the weeks go by, and share it with your children. Adolescents will either worry or feel cut off if you hide your distress and may also believe that they too should hide their upset.
- Try not to idealise a dead parent. Retaining the reality of the person is a comfort. False images may prevent the adolescent from speaking about their loss.
- Avoid statements such as, 'Your dad is watching you from Heaven'. This can make the adolescent obsessively cons- cious of everything they say and do, as if they are being personally observed.
- Remember that adolescents may need to escape with their friends, to go to a disco, to go to the pictures. These activities are not a sign of callousness or lack of caring. They are often

the adolescent's way of coping.

- Maintain gentle controls and discipline. Discipline can be difficult for the adolescent where there is no second opinion, or 'court of appeal', in the house.

- Encourage the adolescent to pursue their normal adolescent activities. Death often makes us more anxious and protective towards all the family. Over-protectiveness is particularly harmful for adolescents in their quest for independence.

- Recognise that the death of a parent can make an adolescent much more worried about the health and welfare of the surviving parent. Try to be reassuring, especially by coming home on time.

- Do not be alarmed if the adolescent produces some difficult behaviour, as time goes by. This may be an expression of their upset.

- Look out for an increase in health concerns. Death makes a young person aware of their own mortality.

- Do not be alarmed if you find that your adolescent son sometimes imitates his father, his laugh, his gestures, talks to his photographs, uses his personal possessions (a daughter might behave similarly after the loss of a mother).

- Inform the school, and ask them to inform you if they have any worries about the adolescent.

- Expect problems with concentration, motivation, learning and studying ability. Studies show that schoolwork can be disrupted for one to two years.

- Be vigilant for signs of depression, such as tearfulness, sadness, change in appetite, change in sleeping pattern, irritability, self-deprecatory remarks, withdrawal, morbid statements, and signs of helplessness.

- Understand that anniversaries, birthdays, Christmas, and all the poignant reminders of the person can re-evoke the pain and loss.

- Do not expect your adolescent to have finished all grieving for at least a year. Remember that we never 'get over' a death, but the pain goes, and good memories remain.

DEATH OF A BROTHER OR SISTER

Research points to the enormity of the loss for an adolescent when a brother or a sister dies. To lose a brother or sister is to lose someone you grew up with, maybe shared a room with, walked home from school with, fought with, and stood up for or colluded with against your parents.

Childhood memories will return; of the pillow fights, the races, the sharing of toys and sweets. If the adolescent is older than the person who died, they may remember the arrival of the new brother or sister and their ambivalent feelings of jealousy and delight.

If the adolescent was younger, they may have followed, pestered, looked up to, copied, loved and hated the now dead sibling. The loss is enormous, whatever the age or whatever the relationship.

Keeping in mind the general guidelines on how to cope after a bereavement, there are also some specific needs to attend to in the grieving adolescent who has lost a bother or sister:

- Make sure that *both* parents break the news.
- Acknowledge the special relationship that exists between brothers and sisters.
- Try to recall an instance in which the surviving adolescent had shown particular kindness or attachment to the deceased child.
- Mention that because it is such a painful loss for you as parents, you might forget, at times, the adolescent's pain.
- Don't idealise the brother or sister who died. The adoles-

cent will lose them again if their memory is turned into sainthood.

- Talk to them about the pain of returning to school without their brother, or the problem of being alone during school breaks without their sister.
- Be aware that the adolescent might benefit from increased attention, and that they might feel guilty about this.
- Consider the pain of an adolescent who continues to live in a bedroom with an empty bed, with possessions strewn about, and having to face the trauma of sorting out these possessions.
- Do not suggest redecorating or removing signs of the dead person too quickly, particularly in a shared bedroom. Let the young person talk about when they might be ready for this.
- Allow the adolescent to know that you do not harbour any anger, blame or reproach if they were in any way involved at the time of death, such as occurs in the event of a tragic car crash when the adolescent was driving.
- Consider that the adolescent may secretly worry that you might prefer that they had died in the place of their brother or sister. Be sensitive to this, and reassure them accordingly.
- Be aware that the adolescent's perspective of life often changes after a brother or sister dies.
- Keep reassuring the adolescent, because research shows that thoughts about a dead sibling may be pervasive, occurring daily, and extending over a long period of time.
- Allow the adolescent to be the principal organiser of the funeral. They will have shared an important generational relationship and may know, if the sibling was close in age, the relevant personal friends, music and flowers that would have been the deceased's choice.
- Remember that allowing the adolescent to organise the

arrangements can be a parting gift to the dead person, and therefore therapeutic for the adolescent.

- Invite the adolescent to involve classmates, perhaps for a guard of honour, to deliver readings, or to sing.
- Allow them to speak at the funeral, if they wish.

DEATH OF A GRANDPARENT

The death of a grandparent is often the first death than a young person encounters. Just because the person is old, may have been ill, or their demise was expected, does not make it any less traumatic.

There can be special levels of understanding between the very young and the very old, and grandparents are often a source of comfort, wisdom and love for young people.

The childhood memories can be overwhelming, with recollections of visits to the grandparent's house, the games played in the garden, holidays spent at their home, or even walks taken with the grandparents.

The adolescent may recollect stories their grandparents told about the past, about the adolescent's parents, producing photograph albums of the parents when they were children, seeing the toys their parents played with, or hearing stories of the past.

Grandparents often have more time than parents to listen to a young person, and they can provide a special kind of love and acceptance of youth. They may have enjoyed a second chance at 'parenting' their grandchildren, and may have done so without the stresses and strains that are present for parents.

The death of a grandparent can, therefore, often represent the end of an era, the end of childhood, or the loss of a special friend. The following are worthwhile suggestions:

- Acknowledge the depth of the grief the adolescent may

feel. Because the adolescent's parents are themselves grieving, the needs of young people can easily be forgotten.

- Speak of the grandparent's particular love for their grandchild, and name the activities they might miss.
- Allow the adolescent to recollect times they spent with the grandparent, stories the grandparent told them, secrets they may have shared.
- Understand that the adolescent may be upset by watching *your* sadness at the loss of your parent. Don't try to protect them by hiding your grief.
- Remember that adolescents observe how you handle your grief. The model you provide is important.
- Consider that the adolescent may feel some relief, especially if a grandparent was cranky due to ill-health. Allow the adolescent to express this emotion without feeling guilty.
- Remember that the death of a grandparent may act as a symbol of the end of childhood. Recognise this, and talk to your child about the meaning of what has just taken place.

DEATH BY SUICIDE

Suicide is a particular kind of death, followed by a particular kind of grief. Suicide seems to defy nature, and the tragedy of the event can be overwhelming because of the belief that it could have been avoided.

Also, while the initial shock is intense, families often retrospectively recall that suicidal intentions had been expressed either directly or indirectly before the act, which can add to the grief, guilt and distress.

The suicide of a parent is especially tragic for a young person, who is likely to feel intense guilt, remorse, anger, embarrassment, rejection, helplessness, confusion, pain, sadness, and fury. It is possible that these emotions will be experienced simultaneously.

It may be helpful to consider the following:

- Make sure that *you* explain what happened, and do not lie to the adolescent. Studies show that telling the truth is best, and that young people who later seek help often do so because of the secrecy and shame that surrounded the death.
- Avoid giving explicit details about the manner of dying. The adolescent should be helped to focus on the loss of the *person* rather than the *manner* of their death.
- Remember that it is crucial to reassure adolescents that this death was not their fault and that nothing they could have done would have prevented it. This is important because of the additional guilt and remorse often experienced after a suicide.
- If the adolescent's behaviour had been especially problematic prior to the parent's death, they may need particular reassurance that the death was not their fault. Explain that parents do not kill themselves just because their children are behaving badly.
- Recognise the danger of a 'copycat' suicide and, if necessary, seek help.
- Remember that professional help is often needed after a suicide because of the trauma experienced by all the family.

DEATH OF A FRIEND

An adolescent who loses a close or 'best' friend will experience enormous grief. Such a death is always highly distressing because the death of any young person contains so many tragic elements.

We must recognise that the adolescent may miss not just a friend but a companion at school, a confidante to share their thoughts, feelings and aspirations with. Likewise, they may have supported each other, fought 'battles' together, fantasised about their futures, and shared the experiences of school, play, and growing up together.

Because of this, there are many particular steps you might take:

- Allow the adolescent plenty of time to talk about their friend. If you knew the friend well, you might mention some funny or interesting things the adolescent and friend did together.
- Encourage them to call to the friend's parents to express their grief. Writing a letter may not just be a comfort to the friend's parents, but will be therapeutic for the adolescent in expressing their loss.
- Be aware that they may need to withdraw from other friends for some time. However, reassure them that it is not a betrayal of their friend if they form other friendships, in time.
- Accompany the adolescent to the funeral, let them buy a bouquet, write a special message, and help them through the formalities of the funeral, which may be new to them.
- If the friend was particularly close and you know the parents, you might ask them sensitively if your child could have a memento. These parents will probably welcome knowing that their son or daughter is being grieved by others.
- Look out for prolonged signs of loneliness, grief or depression. Losing a friend can be intense during adolescence, at a time when emotions are strong.
- Inform the school, particularly if the friend attended another school, so that the teachers will be aware that the adolescent is grieving.

At a time of bereavement, the process of helping adolescents should begin with helping ourselves, thereby ensuring that we have the psychological supports to enable us to attend to the needs of our children.

The suggestions above will help you to help the adolescent to cope. However, we must always remember that there is no one way to deal with death and dying. There are no emotions we 'ought' to feel, there are no reactions we are 'required' to experience.

The grief process is frequently distressing. But, in time, the pain will gradually ease, and the sadness, grief and anguish will be transformed into a series of treasured memories of the person who has died.

EXAMINATION STRESS

IN MANY WAYS, MUCH OF the stress and panic at examination time results from poor preparation. The anxiety about being unprepared may not only arise in the weeks prior to an examination, but may be the result of bad preparation in the months and even years before the event.

Anxiety and panic may be justified because the teenager has failed to develop a proper pattern of study, good study habits, strategies for learning and remembering, ability to concentrate, or experience in communicating knowledge under examination conditions. Being poorly prepared is the greatest precipitator of anxiety and panic.

Studies show that a small measure of stress or anxiety can help motivation, and provide the adrenaline to energise the student to study. However, as anxiety increases, students may feel overwhelmed by the amount of work to be done and lose confidence in their capacity to cope. It is at this point that anxiety and panic interrupt the study and learning process.

The following are the signs and symptoms of anxiety that may interrupt, rather than motivate, the student:

- Poor concentration, being forgetful about homework assignments, being disorganised, mislaying books and pens, and generally being absent-minded.
- General worry, and feeling apprehensive at the thought of study and examinations.
- Feeling overwhelmed, and unable to cope with the amount that needs to be learned.
- Becoming restless, and switching from one task to another without learning anything about either. This may include taking breaks at ten minute intervals, along with paring of

pencils and other distractible behaviours.

- Feeling tired, unwell, and becoming hypochondriacal as an expression of anxiety. (Make sure there is no physical cause for such complaints.)
- Irritability, touchiness, and becoming quick-tempered.
- Feeling inadequate, perceiving that other students are more able, studying more, and feeling helpless to do anything about improving study techniques.
- Having nightmares about 'drying up' at examination time, doing the wrong questions, or failing.
- Problems in falling asleep, with the brain 'racing' over all that has to be studied before the examination.
- Experiencing feelings of depression, sadness, tearfulness, and feelings of worthlessness and hopelessness about it all.
- Being talkative in a pressurised or euphoric way. Getting on a 'high' about what has to be achieved.
- Being unable to relax. Remember that some rest and leisure are very important during examination years, and parents would rightly be concerned by a student who could not take any time off.
- Increased physiological symptoms such as palpitations, chest pains, shortness of breath, yawning, sighing, nausea, diarrhoea, dry mouth, loss of appetite, or increase in appetite.
- Constantly rushing to the toilet, or any kind of incontinence due to stress.
- Tension headaches or migraine, generalised feelings of being tense. Tremor, jerky movements, or blurred vision arising when seriously anxious.
- General aches and muscular pains, clenching of teeth, and skin problems including clammy hands, perspiration, and poor pallor.

Symptoms of examination panic and phobia

Prolonged or excessive anxiety symptoms can build up to an acute point where the student begins to become 'panicked'. In most situations of danger people react by 'fight or flight', where they can either run from the situation or stay and confront it. Panic may occur when the student feels that they are unable to study ('fight') for the imminent examination, and they are also unable to avoid the examination ('flight').

The shift from generalised anxiety about study to acute anxiety and panic about examinations is distressing. Panic is normal if there is a rational reason for it. The student who has not studied may justifiably experience some panic, as the examination approaches. Whether this is turned to good effect or becomes crippling depends on how it arises, why it begins, and how it is managed.

If panicky feelings begin some months prior to the examination, there is still time for the student to break the panic cycle. One of the best ways to get rid of panic is to deal with the symptoms, and this often lies in reassuring the student, helping them to devise study plans, providing necessary additional help or grinds, and implementing the suggestions that are outlined later in this chapter.

It is, however, important to distinguish between what people commonly describe as 'panic' from the symptoms of true panic attack and panic disorder. In some cases, panic may become acute and the student may suffer a panic attack prior to examinations, or even during an examination. The following are the signs and symptoms of such an attack:

- A sudden and unexpected feeling of intense terror.
- Fainting, ringing in the ears, and wishing to vomit.
- Feeling physically overwhelmed. Often, there is a peak of distress which then abates fairly rapidly.

- Sensations of smothering are frequently described, and the person cannot catch their breath. There may be a feeling of choking, which exacerbates the terror.
- The person may tremble or shake, and sweat profusely.
- Experiences of nausea, or abdominal distress.
- Perceptions of being 'outside' themselves, as if they are observing their body.
- Feelings of numbness, or tingling sensations that refuse to go away.
- Terror about dying during the attack.
- Sudden feelings of being chilled, or becoming excessively flushed and hot.
- Fear of totally losing control, and terror at the thought of fleeing the examination room.

Panic attacks that arise in the months before examinations require medical intervention, removal of pressure and anxiety, psychological support, training in relaxation techniques, coping strategies, and a comprehensive plan to assist the student through the study and examination process.

Furthermore, anticipatory panic can leave the adolescent fearing a 'panic attack' during the examination. This can result in 'examination phobia'. Since it is important that the student does not become phobic about the examination, action should be taken to ensure that the teenager does not slide into this condition.

Such feelings are exceptionally distressing, and require professional intervention and help.

STUDY PROBLEMS
Teenagers frequently do not study because they do not know *how* to study. Their difficulty can be misinterpreted as laziness or lack of application. In fact, most young people want to do

well at school and in examinations. In one Irish study of teen-agers (12–15 years), over 80% said that they feel proud of them-selves when they do well in school. Indeed, in that survey, doing well at school rated as one of their most important sources of pride and self-esteem.

Studying is difficult if the teenager does not know how to go about it. Additionally, it is difficult if they cannot evaluate what they have learned or if they believe that they are not retaining the information. Time spent unproductively can make young people restless, distractible, demotivated, and cause them to lose heart.

It is when we feel helpless or overwhelmed that anxiety in-creases. As the anxiety increases, learning decreases. Anxiety about examinations, therefore, arises in many young people for the following reasons:

- They do not know exactly *what* they are meant to know.
- They do not know *how* to learn.
- They have not chosen a *place* to study.
- They have not learned *techniques* of revision.
- They have no examination *strategies*.
- They have specific *learning problems*.

Parents can be enormously helpful to teenagers by helping them overcome the above obstacles, and by providing the physical, psychological and practical conditions that favour good study.

KNOWING WHAT TO LEARN
- Make sure the young person is clear about exactly what they are expected to know in any subject. Having to study history sounds daunting, whereas a plan involving the study of a chapter of history per week is comprehensible

and manageable. This turns general or free-floating anxiety into specific tasks to be solved.

- Encourage them to draw up a study plan using a 'page per day' diary, in which they list all their activities, including leisure time, homework requirements for each day, and small defined pieces of revision in chosen subjects.

- As the examination approaches, help them to refine this plan by counting the number of study days left, the number of subjects to be taken in the examination, and the division of their time to allow revision of each of these subjects.

- A week before the examination, they should have a specific countdown plan for each day of the week.

- It is suggested that four days before the examination they specifically concentrate on the material for the *second* subject they are sitting.

- The two days prior to the examination should be spent almost entirely on the *first* subject they will be sitting.

KNOWING HOW TO LEARN

Knowing how to learn involves knowing the medium through which you learn best. For some people this is by *reading*; for others it is by *writing notes*. Some people prefer to *hear* the material. Others prefer to *see* the material in a visual display.

- Help your teenager to decide which medium best facilitates their learning.

- Encourage them to experiment with different learning methods, e.g., reading, listening, drawing, etc.

- Remind them that note-taking can be visual, and diagrams, mind-maps, etc., can be effective. Long pages of text may be less effective in providing memory cues.

- Index cards are helpful, particularly for topic headings.

Diagrams can be used for revision the night before an examination.

- If the adolescent prefers to *hear* material, use of a dictaphone or a tape recorder can be helpful.

- Encourage the adolescent to organise their study time as efficiently as possible. This will minimise time-wasting, and will ensure that the teenager is as fresh and focused as possible.

- Restrict phone calls from friends to specified times, so that study will not be repeatedly interrupted.

- Suggest that music is listened to at particular times of the day, not during homework.

- Be flexible about the time when young people study. Don't pressurise your teenager to study only at set times. As long as the work is done, that is what matters.

- Remember that some people like to get up early in the morning to study. Others prefer to study later at night. The 'larks' and 'owls' have different patterns of study which ought to be accommodated.

- Colour-coding different subjects may help the ordering of material, and will therefore be a help to memory. Suggest that the adolescent decides on a colour that they will always associate with a particular subject, e.g., blue for English, green for Irish, etc. Textbooks could be papered in these colours, and accompanying folders should maintain the same colour-code.

- Remind them that examination success does not just depend on *what* you know but on *how you communicate* this knowledge: clearly, succinctly and within the examination time limit. Practising providing answers, and timing themselves on answers, helps the young person to measure their written communicative ability.

- Encourage them to read over what they have written, to

check for spelling errors and punctuation. Reading aloud often demonstrates whether a sentence is unwieldy or whether it makes sense.

- Advise them about the usefulness of short sentences and paragraphs.
- Recommend that the adolescent uses an alphabetically indexed notebook in which they can write words that they regularly spell incorrectly. Most people repeatedly spell the same words incorrectly. The notebook can be used as a quick reference.
- Suggest that they read newspaper articles, listen to radio programmes, and analyse the ways in which information is conveyed.
- Help them to consider current topics or debates which may be potential topics in examination essays.
- Suggest that the adolescent decides on opening sentences or paragraphs to use in essays. These could be kept in an alphabetically indexed notebook, and revised or added to as additional points or ideas emerge.
- Avoid the temptation to 'do' the adolescents' homework for them. Study is *their* responsibility, and you won't be there on the day of the examination.

CHOOSING A PLACE TO STUDY

The physical surroundings and conditions in which we study are important. Order, peace, quiet, and warm (not stuffy) conditions are best. Parents can help by providing the conditions that will optimise study, and the following suggestions may be useful:

- Help the adolescent to organise a specific place to study, such as a small spare room or the adolescent's bedroom.
- Try to make the study area inviting and attractive.

- Try to minimise the distraction of television by keeping the volume low. Televisions in bedrooms or study areas are obviously not advisable.
- Provide a desk and some shelves, and a comfortable chair to sit on.
- Suggest that they use containers for pens, rulers, compass, paper-clips, erasers, etc. Having an available supply avoids distracting trips around the house.
- Keep a supply of refill pads, notebooks, and other materials, so that time is not wasted when new ones are required.
- Provide files for notes under subject headings. One large folder per subject often helps the young person to keep their papers segregated and tidy.
- Ensure that lighting is sufficient.
- Some people find that lighting a candle, or burning essential oils, helps concentration. Advise on safety, however, and remind them that lighted candles should never be left unattended.

TECHNIQUES AND STRATEGIES FOR EXAMINATIONS

Having divided study into manageable segments, having decided on the best learning techniques, and having created the ideal working conditions, it is important that the young person demonstrates their knowledge in the actual examination. The following advice may be useful:

- Remind them to be physically comfortable during the examination by visiting the toilet beforehand, having some boiled sweets (not in noisy wrappers) to suck during the examination, a soft drink or glucose drink for energy (if allowed), and having handkerchiefs available.
- Remind them to always read the questions. Then read them *again*. Many young people lose marks because they

139

answer questions that were not asked.

- Suggest that they read the entire paper before rushing into answering a question. Sometimes, young people finish a question only to discover that a later question requires information they have already given.

- Encourage them to plan their time with precision and to stop when the allocated time for each question is up. Examiners often have to wade through pages of detail on early questions, with little or no information provided on the last questions.

- Suggest that the adolescent scribbles down any ideas for further questions as they come to mind. Writing a key word will ensure that they do not forget to make these points when they come to the question.

- Help them to analyse the terminology used in examination papers, and help them to know precisely what each phrase means, e.g., 'discuss', 'describe', 'define', 'distinguish between'. They all have different meanings and require different responses.

- Advise them to read instructions carefully, such as 'choose one of the following'. Teenagers often lose examination time by doing more questions than required and are left with insufficient time to finish the paper.

- Make sure they have all the necessary implements, such as spare pens, etc., for the examination.

SPECIFIC LEARNING PROBLEMS

Much of the distress that young people may experience with regard to school can be avoided by observing the signs of difficulties at school. Monitoring school progress from the earliest age will help parents to discover if their child has learning problems, and the following signs are significant:

- Spending too little time, or too much time, doing home-work.
- Resisting getting down to homework. This may not be due to laziness; it may be that the task is too difficult or intellectually daunting.
- Avoiding school, developing 'Monday morning' illnesses, school refusal, or school truancy.
- Complaining about teachers going too fast, being too cross, or not explaining enough. Check this out, as it may be that the young person is simply unable to keep up.
- Becoming irritable, angry, and disruptive in relation to schoolwork, but not showing these signs at other times.
- Achieving poor results on an ongoing basis.
- Attaining very high results in some subjects and very poor results in others. In this case, consider the possibility of a specific problem, e.g., never being able to understand maths may be a sign of a specific maths disorder.
- Demonstrating problems in literacy. A Department of Education research paper suggests that 23% of Junior-cycle students are unable to cope with the demands of Post-Primary literacy.
- Showing signs of what is known as Written Language Disorder. This disorder includes specific and persistent difficulties with reading, spelling and writing, although intelligence will have been assessed as normal. These difficulties stand in stark contrast to development and ability in other areas, but they interfere with performance at school.
- Demonstrating problems in reading aloud, in recognising or breaking down words, introducing mispronunciations or word substitutions, e.g., reading 'furious' for 'ferocious'. Using additional words, or omitting words, could also be a sign that your teenager may have a specific problem.
- Showing specific spelling difficulties. Analysis can show if

these are caused by auditory (hearing) or visual (sight or perception) problems.

- Not taking in what has been studied or read. This is one of the most insidious problems in that the young person reads aloud with ease but fails to absorb information.

- Demonstrating poor writing skills. This may involve problems in assessing ideas pertinent to a topic, difficulty with the organisation and layout of ideas within a topic, errors in word choice, or very confused use of punctuation.

- Getting into trouble for poor or untidy writing, or being reluctant to write. A Written Language Disorder may be apparent if the young person has poor pencil grip and letter formation, chronically slow writing, or a tendency to produce a minimum of written quantity despite time and effort.

- Being described as lazy, untidy, lacking in motivation. Again, consider the possibility of a Written Language Disorder.

- Getting into trouble for poor answers, silly answers, or not responding to questions appropriately. Remember that written language disorders are often accompanied by a disorder in general language skills.

- Demonstrating language problems, such as misunderstanding grammatical forms, not comprehending instructions, using sentences that are fragmented and that do not convey their message, having word retrieval problems, being unable to give directions, or being unable to ask questions.

- Being accused of cheekiness, bad attitude, insolence. Young people with language disorders can have problems with non-verbal communication. They may violate the rules of normal communication, such as misinterpreting facial expressions, encroaching on body space or personal space, presenting inappropriate facial expressions, being happy in a sad situation, or leering when being reprimanded.

- Being unable to cope academically. Consider that the problem may be more serious than lack of motivation. Psychological assessment is advised, if you are concerned.

Young people need special support during examinations, particularly those examinations that extend over two or three weeks. If they are studying hard, trying to cope with anxiety, staying up late revising, eating in a hurried fashion, and ruminating about the mistakes made on papers, they need particular support and guidance during this time. The following are some suggestions to help them through the process:

- Make life as easy for adolescents as possible during examinations. This is not the time to take them to task about untidy rooms, appearance, or behaviour.
- Show the young person that you support them and that you are sympathetic towards them during this stressful time.
- Irritability and anger are often expressions of the stress of examinations. Don't react angrily if the teenager shows these emotions. You should respond by acknowledging how 'edgy' they must be feeling, and ask if you can help.
- Relieve them of any household work. Their task at this time is study, not housework.
- Provide clean clothes for them to wear each day. It adds to the tension if they are searching for clothes before an examination.
- Give them a 'Good luck' card with a personal note. A message that conveys that you admire their work and commitment to date, not one that anticipates success, is reassuring.
- Don't promise monetary rewards (bribes) for success. Study is their privilege and responsibility.
- If you wish to reward examination efforts, provide a re-

143

ward prior to the examination for the study they have done. Often, young people are promised substantial amounts per subject, which adds to the tension.

- Try to get up especially early, and prepare a nourishing breakfast.

- If they are going in for an afternoon examination, help them to get up at a reasonable hour in the morning. Also, prepare a very light lunch; heavy food in the middle of the day causes drowsiness in the afternoon.

- Prepare an appetising and nourishing dinner, and eat with them. Left to themselves, they may snack badly, and 'junk food' at this time does not help health or concentration.

- If possible, drive them to school in plenty of time. They do not need the anxiety of waiting for buses, being alone before the examination at a bus stop, or the fear of being late for the examination.

- Bring them shopping several weeks before the examination and buy new pens, pencils and any other requirements. However, it takes time to 'run in' many pens, so favoured pens should not be changed.

- Provide large folders for each subject, into which they can put notes, additional information, revision work and last minute revision cards. Order and neatness will help concentration and create order in thinking. An array of scattered papers around the room only causes confusion.

- Encourage them not to ruminate on previous tests they have completed. However, allow them to talk about these tests if they are anxious.

- Help them, after each examination, to set aside the books, notes and folders they no longer need. Preferably remove them from the room in which they are studying. This will get rid of the temptation to check up on answers or 'mistakes' they made in the last test.

- It is not advisable to ask them for the precise answers they gave to questions. If they choose to tell you, be encouraging but do not point out mistakes.
- If the adolescent tells you that they made a major time error and did not complete an examination, do not be angry. Suggest that this is an important lesson and that they will not make that error for the rest of the examination. Remind them that almost everyone, at some stage, makes this mistake and learns from it.
- If they think they have done badly, remarks such as, 'How could you not have read the question correctly?' are not helpful. Remarks such as, 'I'm sorry you did not get the chance to show all you know' or, 'Most people have a paper that goes wrong for them' are more useful.
- Encourage them to take a break (a walk, a shower, watch television), so that they can 'let go' of the last examination before moving on to the next.
- If they do badly on a paper in a preferred subject, acknowledge that this is disappointing. However, ask them to consider that their expectations may be very high for that paper and they still may have done well relative to others. Point out that it is good that they know so much about the subject, even if they did not get to show all their knowledge.
- Do not project your anxiety on to them. Don't greet them on return from examinations with anxious questions about how they performed. Ask how they feel, not how well they did.
- While they are out at the examination, tidy the adolescent's study room, and make it pleasant to return to. Make sure not to disturb notes that may be laid out in a particular order.
- Provide alternatives to tea or coffee or any other liquid

stimulants before bed. The old fashioned glass of warm milk is ideal, and flavoured additives are pleasant.

- Try to get brothers and sisters to respect the adolescent's need for peace and quiet.
- When they take a short break from study, encourage brothers and sisters to be considerate, such as allowing the adolescent their choice of television viewing. However, don't make the home so unnatural that their anxiety increases.
- Try to ensure that the period during their examination is not one of stress for you. This is not the time for parents to be under pressure at work. This may need some advance planning.
- Avoid any family arguments, which may be upsetting and stressful.
- Don't forbid them to stay up a bit later if they are anxious to revise. However, point out that the brain needs some rest to be active the next day.
- Treat their examinations seriously, but not anxiously. Remember that there are many alternative routes for the adolescent to achieve their vocational choices. Set-backs in examinations may be worrying, but they are not life-threatening.

Disturbed Behaviour

GROWING UP OFTEN INVOLVES TRANSIENT emotional and behavioural problems. Indeed, many of the normal teenage behaviours can appear to be signs of disturbance when, in fact, they are simply part of an adolescent stage.

It would be easy to misinterpret some teenage behaviours as signs of disturbance, or even as signs of psychiatric disorder. These behaviours could include: wearing black teeshirts, favouring funereal music, indulging in extensive body-piercing, or having hairstyles that involve irregular or total shaving of the head.

The adolescent may also provide monosyllabic responses, suffer apparently uncontrollable mood swings, engage in outbursts of irrationality, withdraw to the bedroom for long periods, express morbid ideas, or make dim prophecies about the future of the planet.

Should these occur, a parent may indeed become worried and believe that the adolescent is going through a phase of significant emotional and behavioural difficulty. However, these behavioural patterns may merely signify that the young person is taking their adolescent 'rebellious' role too seriously.

It is, therefore, important for parents to be able to distinguish between the 'normal' signs of turbulence, and signs of a more troubled adolescence.

THE TROUBLESOME ADOLESCENT
Behavioural problems are much more common in boys than in girls, particularly behaviour that causes social disapproval. It is estimated that there are 3–4 boys for every girl with conduct problems. Sometimes, such problems appear in childhood and

continue into adolescence. In other cases, the first signs of difficulty arise during the adolescent years.

Behaviour or conduct problems are distinguished by the degree of aggressive and disruptive behaviour. Sometimes, these behaviours are carried out within the peer group. At other times, the behaviours involve the adolescent lying or stealing at home, or bullying and being disruptive at school. Sometimes, all of these problems may occur together. Signs that a young person is in difficulty and unable to control their conduct include:

- General disobedience and defiance at home of a more challenging and ongoing nature than a parent would expect.
- Problems of bullying, with parents receiving reports from school or from other parents about their adolescent behaving in a cruel, taunting or unkind fashion towards others.
- Difficulties in telling the truth, and finding out that the teenager is often lying about major or even minor issues. Such lies may be about where the adolescent has been, with whom the adolescent has spent the evening, or how the time was spent.
- Fighting at home with brothers or sisters, fighting with other adolescents, or being generally aggressive and arrogant.
- Constantly threatening to 'run away' from home, or actually doing so.
- Refusing to go to school, and becoming extremely upset, with bouts of anger and violence, if forced to attend.
- Playing truant from school, or teachers reporting disruptive or attention-seeking behaviour in the classroom.
- Aggressive outbursts during class, in which the young person may be verbally abusive to the teacher or even become physically threatening.

- Stealing money at home or from others.
- Solitary behaviour, rejecting company, rejecting conversation with parents, and being unwilling to communicate with others in any positive manner.

DELINQUENT BEHAVIOUR

Delinquency is a special category because it involves breaking the law. Both conduct problems and problems of delinquency are more pronounced among boys than girls, with the relative ratios for delinquent behaviour estimated to be as high as ten to one. However, recent studies suggest that the rate of increase in delinquency among girls is rising much faster than the rate of increase among boys. Most signs of delinquency are obvious, but some are less so. Look out for the following:

- Experiencing inability to express emotions in non-aggressive ways. Failing to distinguish between what is acceptable behaviour and what is unacceptable.
- Having poor social skills and exceptionally poor self-esteem, leading to a denial and dismissal of societal rules.
- Knowing that behaviour is unacceptable but being unable to control it. Alternatively, being able to control the behaviour but choosing not to.
- Feeling socially or economically deprived and resentful of the possessions of others. Experiencing injustice in the distribution of wealth, and deciding to take what appears to the adolescent to be justifiably due to them.
- Feeling worthless, without any future in life, rejected by the educational system, and feeling confined by dismal physical and social surroundings.
- Intentionally eliciting a parent's attention, concern or anger, or 'revenging' a parent for harsh discipline or emotional hurt by committing acts that embarrass the parent.

- Emulating models of violence from media, film and video, which depict gratuitous aggression. Looking up to aggressive, violent, or criminal models in the community.

- Being bored, having nothing to do, and having no acceptable outlets for energy.

- Carrying out acts of vandalism, defacing public property, drawing graffiti, breaking public lighting, damaging bus-stops or seats, etc.

- Demonstrating reckless behaviour when in the company of peers, such as scattering litter, being noisy or ill-behaved on the street, in buses, or in public.

- Showing poor understanding of the serious risks involved in unruly activity, particularly the risk of becoming involved in delinquent behaviour.

- Experiencing inability to delay gratification. Being impulsive, needy, and unable to control wishes and wants.

- Engaging in shoplifting for personal gain, or, more seriously, as part of an organised activity to sell stolen goods.

- Setting fires, particularly fires in buildings, schools, government offices. It is worth noting that adolescents who feel that a system has failed them (e.g., school) may show their rejection by trying to vandalise or destroy the system.

- Damaging cars, stealing cars, and 'joyriding'.

- Taking and selling illegal drugs. Becoming addicted to drugs or alcohol, and stealing goods or selling drugs to finance such addictions.

- Being violent to innocent citizens. Being verbally abusive, physically threatening, or physically aggressive.

- Coming into contact with 'the law', and being apprehended, arrested, or charged with criminal activity.

EMOTIONAL PROBLEMS

While some adolescents cause their parents to be concerned because of their increasingly negative anti-social or delinquent behaviour, others invite parental concern due to behavioural signs of being emotionally troubled. The adolescent may appear to parents to be excessively anxious, perfectionistic, obsessional, ritualistic, compulsive, socially withdrawn, panicky, hysterical, or depressed.

The many tasks of adolescence can arouse great anxiety in young people, and we should not be surprised, therefore, that the first signs that a young person is emotionally troubled or anxious arise during the adolescent stage.

It is of great concern to parents if their children develop anxieties, show troubled behaviour or become depressed, and parents are often unsure if a particular behaviour is a sign that the adolescent is distressed. The following signs and symptoms are worth looking out for:

SIGNS OF ACUTE ANXIETY

Sometimes, anxiety is shown in young people through ritualistic, obsessive or compulsive behaviour. Indeed, it is estimated that approximately 60% of those who show their anxiety in this way are adolescents or young adults. Also, this is more common in boys than girls during adolescence, whereas both men and women suffer this problem more equally in adulthood. The following are signs of this particular anxiety, which is known as Obsessive Compulsive Disorder:

- Being excessively distressed, and the disturbance extending to more and more areas, including health, safety, general thoughts, and social situations.
- Repeated washing of hands, scrubbing with disinfectant, and extreme annoyance when asked to desist.

151

- Ritualistic behaviours, such as requiring that everyone in the family be seated at the same time, that objects are touched a set number of times before being used, or that the bed is remade before getting into it.
- Being perfectionistic, and worrying about the consequences of not repeatedly checking. For example, having to empty the schoolbag and check and recheck that all the schoolbooks are present.
- Fearing that some disaster will occur if precautions such as checking and counting are not taken. Engaging in magical thinking about the power of these behaviours.
- Needing to have everything organised in a certain way, perfectly symmetrical, in a straight line, absolutely balanced.
- Feeling compelled to carry out tasks in a certain order. As an example, the adolescent may feel compelled to brush their teeth before combing their hair.
- Fearing contamination from other people, causing a fear of shaking hands. Wearing gloves, to avoid physical contact with others.
- Being fearful of using telephones, afraid of being contaminated by radiation, worrying about germs. Covering or protecting the hands before contact with specific objects.
- Fearing that family members may become ill through contamination.
- Expressing inappropriate guilt, embarrassment, or sense of shame.
- Experiencing great doubt. For example, the adolescent may repeatedly fear that they have injured someone.
- Repetitive thoughts of violence, which will not go away or be relieved.
- Thoughts of committing a terrible act. The adolescent begins to believe that these thoughts should be severely punished.

HYPOCHONDRIASIS

Adolescents sometimes express their anxiety by becoming pre-occupied with physical or health concerns. Often, these worries focus on the possibility of contracting an illness, rather than on the delusion that an illness is present. Sometimes, however, there can be the false belief that there is disfigurement or a hidden illness present. Also, psychological problems manifest themselves in disorders such as anorexia, bulimia and obesity, in addition to hysteria.

Physical symptoms may develop as an unconscious means of avoiding a situation. Symptoms may also be the physical outcome of prolonged stress and anxiety. Of course, the possibility of a real illness should always be investigated before it is assumed that health worries are psychological or psychosomatic in origin.

The following may be signs of excessive health concerns:

- Exaggerated worries about illness, such as vague aches, headaches, tummy upsets, or back problems.
- General aching of muscles (often caused by tension and anxiety).
- Complaints about nausea, vomiting, or diarrhoea.
- Concern about contracting a serious illness, developing cancer, contracting AIDS, or having a heart attack.
- Belief that a part of the body, for example the face, is grossly unattractive or disfigured, when objectively it would not appear to be so. The adolescent cannot be reassured about this.

HYSTERICAL REACTIONS

Hysteria occurs when emotions are exaggerated or uncontrolled. For example, hysteria may occur at pop concerts where the uncontrolled emotions become contagious. On the other hand, hysteria may manifest itself in specific physical symptoms, e.g., when a person finds that they lose power in any body part following a traumatic event. Likewise, a preferred writing hand may become a symbol for the fear of a written examination, and therefore become 'paralysed'. The possibility of a medical cause for such hysteria *always* needs to be investigated.

Signs to look out for are as follows:

- Sudden complaints about paralysis, e.g., in an arm or a leg.
- Loss of sensation in parts of the body.
- Difficulties in swallowing, or being unable to swallow. This may lead to refusal to take food.
- Complaints about chest pains or constriction of the heart. This could occur after the death of a parent from a heart attack, and may be a symbol of the adolescent's grief reaction.

FEELINGS OF PANIC

It is not unusual for adolescents to experience panic, particularly after a family illness or death, a road traffic accident, or some other traumatic event. Examinations can also be a source of panic. Furthermore, the many social demands of fitting in with the peer group can panic adolescents to the point where they become phobic about such encounters. Girls are more likely to panic than boys. This becomes particularly true in adulthood, when panic disorder is more associated with women.

The symptoms of panic are as follows:

- Feelings of nausea, choking, trembling, palpitations, sweating, tightness in the chest.
- Dizziness, or feeling faint.
- A feeling of impending doom, and a fear of dying.
- Tingling sensations, shortness of breath, smothering sen-

sations.

- Fearing that the person is 'losing their mind' or 'going crazy'.
- Fearing leaving the house, or becoming involved in social events, in case panic might occur.

UNHAPPINESS AND DEPRESSION

Depression in adolescence is not uncommon. The young person can become overwhelmed by the problems of growing up and may find it hard to cope. There is a tendency for a greater proportion of girls than boys to show signs of being depressed, particularly as adolescence progresses. However, adolescent boys tend to enact their depression in destructive behaviour or in a mixture of conduct and emotional problems. Signs of depression include the following:

- Feeling sad, tearful, 'down', and being unable to shake off these sad and depressed feelings.
- Losing all interest in things that previously were sought out and enjoyed.
- Feeling worthless and guilty, helpless and hopeless.
- Losing appetite, or being unable to resist food.
- Experiencing problems sleeping. The adolescent may complain that they wake up exceptionally early and cannot return to sleep.
- Feeling excessively tired and lacking in energy. Alternatively, being restless, unable to sit still, and wanting to be active all the time.
- Experiencing problems with concentration, poor application to schoolwork, or diminished memory for lessons just learnt. The adolescent may also complain that decisions are difficult to make.
- The adolescent may think of death in a welcoming way, and might even consider suicide and how it would be

accomplished.

MORE SERIOUS EMOTIONAL PROBLEMS IN ADOLESCENCE

Emotional problems in adolescence are sometimes difficult to distinguish from serious and incapacitating disorders. What happens when the early anxieties, angers and rages, health fears, obsessive behaviours, thoughts and compulsive actions, social anxiety and poor social skill, anti-social behaviour, hysteria or depression come to take on another and more serious meaning?

Parents will worry that the emotional disorder is striking at the very foundations of the adolescent's personality. Parents will also struggle with fears that the adolescent may suffer serious and lifelong consequences. Such concerns may be justified, given that the symptoms could signal the onset of schizophrenia. This is an illness that affects one out of every 100 in the population, and the symptoms should be taken seriously.

It is unusual to see a *peak* of these symptoms before the age of 20, although many signs may appear in adolescence and progressive deterioration may be evident. Onset tends to be earlier in men than in women, and more males than females may be affected.

The signs that a young person may be suffering from schizophrenia, and in serious need of help, include the following:

- High levels of anxiety, poor emotional control, and unpredictable outbursts of rage or violence dating back to childhood.
- A history of anti-social behaviour, particularly towards the family. Also, great dependence on the family, and feelings of depression.
- Great anger at being forced to get out of bed in the morning. Anger at being forced to become involved in activities. Apart from these angry outbursts, there may be great

apathy.

- Rejection by peers, being left alone at school, and being considered odd or eccentric.
- An early pattern of seeking seclusion, being secretive, exhibiting symptoms of shyness and disinterest in surroundings, retreating into the inner world of imagination and fantasy.
- Great loneliness and isolation. Poor self-esteem and low confidence.
- Using unusual speech or language patterns that are hard to understand, or that are odd or incomprehensible. Using words that rhyme, or 'echoing' back words that have just been spoken.
- Creating drawings which are bizarre or excessively morbid.
- A significant decrease in academic performance, or a steady deterioration in ability.
- Attaching unnecessary significance or meaning to innocent acts by others.
- Blunting of emotions, lack of drive, eccentric behaviour.
- Outbursts of giggling or laughing, and a childishness in responses.
- Believing that one's thoughts can be heard (thought broadcasting).
- Believing that one's thoughts are being taken away by others (thought withdrawal).
- Fearing that thoughts are being put into the adolescent's head (thought insertion).
- Believing that others are in control of one's thoughts.
- Hearing voices which are in the third person (auditory hallucinations). The voices may appear to be discussing or arguing about the person, and referring to the adolescent by name or as 'he' or 'she'.
- Believing that they are possessed by aliens, by evil spirits,

or by other figures in the community. Attributing their actions to control or manipulation by others.

- Experiencing frightening, intense, vivid hallucinations. Experiencing unusual and bizarre perceptions.
- Living in a different 'reality', and viewing the world in a strange way.
- Believing that there is something wrong with a body part.
- Delusional belief in a disfigurement, despite evidence to the contrary.
- Being restless, and pacing at night. Alternatively, being withdrawn and non-communicative .
- Being locked in a world of fragmented thoughts.

WHAT CAN PARENTS DO?

Disorders of behaviour and conduct, delinquent acts, and the vast range of emotional concerns and difficulties encountered by adolescents require very particular attention. However, remember that the majority of young people actually negotiate the adolescent process well, in a good relationship with their parents, with reasonable emotional control, and with successful integration into the adult world.

It is only in sad and rare instances that adolescents transgress behaviourally or emotionally across boundaries that are psychologically threatening or medically serious. What we need to do, as parents, can be ascertained from many other chapters in this book. However, in general terms, we can help young people by considering the following:

- Talk to your adolescent about what is wrong.
- Open channels of communication, to allow for discussion.
- Don't be panicked into overreaction. Remember that behavioural change is part of the adolescent process. It is only when it gets out of control that it requires intervention.

- In the event of persistent and worrying difficulties and disorders, consult your doctor and get immediate professional help.

DEPRESSION AND SUICIDE

DEPRESSION IS OFTEN CONFUSED WITH the normal symptoms of adolescence. This confusion can lead to two unfortunate outcomes. Firstly, we may mistakenly interpret some of the normal, temporary moods and behaviours of adolescence as signs of depression. More seriously, we may miss the real signs of depression and attribute them to just another adolescent phase.

It is clear that depression is a disabling condition that can seriously disrupt the adolescent process. However, depression can be difficult to identify, and it is not surprising that parents become confused by the overlap between the characteristics of growing up and the signs of depression.

Furthermore, the somewhat fluid and unsettled process of teenage development can lead young people to mask their underlying depressive moods in a range of disguises, such as restlessness, behavioural problems, and health or hypochondriacal concerns.

Additionally, defining depression is particularly difficult because the word has become misused. It can mean anything from feeling a bit down or unhappy, to a mental disorder that can require immediate hospitalisation, and may even lead to a young person taking their own life.

It is imperative, therefore, that we understand where normal unhappiness ends and depression as a disorder begins. Yet, this is further complicated by the fact that several different types of depression have been identified. In simple and broad terms, these include the following:

- *Reactive depression:* This is the most common form of depression. It usually arises as a reaction to a loss or a traumatic event, or as a response to a variety of situations that cause an adolescent to be unhappy or distressed.

- *Endogenous/Biological depression:* This form of depression normally has more biological origins and less immediate environmental triggers. As a result, there is often no discernible or apparent cause.
- *Manic depression:* In this case, the adolescents may experience elation or depression, or, in some cases, may swing from manic to depressed states.

THE SYMPTOMS OF DEPRESSION

The *type*, the *intensity* and the *duration* of symptoms are key factors in drawing a distinction between adolescent unhappiness and adolescent depression. If depression is a dominant mood, rather than a transitory distress, we would be right to be concerned. The following are symptoms to watch out for:

- Feeling great sadness, looking sad, rarely smiling, feeling flat and apathetic.
- Feeling sadder in the morning, with mood improving during the day. Conversely, in some depressions, the person may become more unhappy as the day progresses.
- Strong feelings of loss, and believing that nothing will ever be right again.
- Tearfulness and crying, being sensitive, easily hurt or insulted, and appearing on the verge of tears.
- Loss of interest in many previously enjoyed activities, or, conversely, a constant search for new activities.
- Restlessness, boredom, finding it difficult to be alone.
- Engaging in dangerous and wild behaviour, using alcohol, taking drugs, or becoming sexually promiscuous. Seeking release from unhappiness by searching for love in such behaviours.

- Retreating to the bedroom, withdrawing from others, wanting to be left alone but also feeling lonely and unwanted.
- Having a very negative view of self, self-deprecation, poor self-esteem and low self-confidence.
- Feeling worthless and hopeless, focusing on real or imagined failures. These may be accompanied by delusions of sin, guilt, unworthiness, illness, or poverty.
- Being morbidly preoccupied with thoughts of death. Ruminating about disease, and expressing many hypochondriacal concerns.
- Feeling tired, having no energy, shuffling, or slouching. In more serious states, there may be a general slowing up of movements, hand-wringing, or monotonous rocking.
- Experiencing oneself as unreal, or everything around one as unreal.
- Difficulty going asleep (initial insomnia), or waking up early and being unable to go back to sleep. This early morning waking (terminal insomnia) may be a sign of endogenous depression.
- Irritability, techiness, finding conversation irksome, being vague and indecisive in conversation, and feeling that life is out of control.
- Neglecting appearance, or taking poor care of personal hygiene.
- Difficulties in concentration, poor attention, problems making decisions and making judgements.
- Loss of weight, loss of appetite, a disinterest in food (especially prevalent in endogenous depression). Compensatory and comfort overeating (more usual in reactive depression).
- Uncertainties about others, feeling suspicious (paranoid ideas), and thinking that other people may wish to inflict

162

some punishment or retribution for imagined misdeeds.

Depression is a condition that covers many degrees, grades and levels of severity, with many precipitating factors involved. Sometimes, there is a predisposition which can be triggered by something that happens to the adolescent. Other times, there is no discernible reason, but this does not mean that the adolescent is not depressed.

It can be difficult for parents to know if their adolescent is merely 'fed up' or is suffering from depression, because the teenage years are characterised by extremes. These highs and lows of adolescence can cause parents and young people to swing on an emotional 'see-saw' that makes it hard to tell whether the adolescent is 'up' or 'down', at any one given moment.

The grades of depression can range from mild to moderate to severe, and may even be life-threatening. The symptoms may be transitory and disappear in a short time. Alternatively, the symptoms may be more prolonged, requiring professional intervention, or, in the case of major or chronic depression, careful medical and psychological management will be required.

It is worthwhile examining the different grades of depression in detail to help you decide what your adolescent might be experiencing and what help they might need.

NORMAL ADOLESCENT DIFFICULTIES
The following are the typical annoyances and difficulties that a young person has to face, which can make them feel 'down':

- Breaking out in spots, or developing severe, lumpy, scarring or disfiguring acne.
- Believing that everyone else is better looking than you are.

Worrying that you are ugly and will remain so.

- Having to wear glasses, or having to wear braces that are uncomfortable or unsightly.
- Having a stammer or a stutter, and discovering that this is more pronounced when nervous or trying to impress.
- Finding it hard to ask parents for money, and having to depend on their moods and generosity for every penny. Believing that your friends have more money or possessions than you have.
- Thinking that you do not have enough clothes, or the right kind of clothes, or that you never look as nice as your friends.
- Finding it hard to keep up in school, and finding the work academically difficult. Being disappointed in your results, or finding that parents are angry about your lack of progress.
- Worrying about examinations, dreading the Junior Certificate or the Leaving Certificate. Fearing that all your future choices depend on your 'points' in the Leaving Certificate.
- Not receiving recognition for your best efforts, finding it difficult to study, or never getting good results despite your efforts.
- Having to carry heavy books to and from school, forgetting required books or assignments, and finding school attendance a daily burden.
- Having to cope with the onset of menstruation (periods), feeling cramps, pain, headaches, backache, and emotional discomfort. Not wanting to participate in sports or physical education at this time, and feeling that you are not receiving enough sympathy.
- Coping with premenstrual tension, feeling depressed, irritable, anxious and awkward, and feeling that nobody understands your stress.

- Experiencing embarrassment caused by changed physical appearance (the appearance of breasts), and being frightened if these changes are remarked on or referred to with sexual innuendo by others.
- Being surprised by uncontrolled erections, initial ejaculation and nocturnal emissions (wet dreams), and being embarrassed by not being able to control these responses.
- Being embarrassed by voice changes, and becoming upset if anyone remarks on, or mimics, the changes in pitch.
- Waiting for facial hair to grow, and not shaving when all your friends seem to do so.
- Being afraid that you are too tall (females), and that you are 'gross', 'monstrous' and 'awkward'. Worrying that boys who are shorter than you will not go out with you.
- Being afraid that you are too small and slight (males), and that you are 'weedy', 'girlish', or a 'wimp'. Feeling less mature, less 'macho', and less advanced than your friends.
- Feeling that life will never be stable or easy, and experiencing overwhelming feelings of stress.
- Wanting to be grown up and wanting to be a child. Not knowing what you want to be.

MORE SERIOUS ADOLESCENT DISTRESSES

Many of the normal adolescent difficulties listed above can be experienced at different times, with varying intensity and duration, and with different levels of frequency. Additionally, the difficulties may be experienced separately or together, and may be encountered at different times during adolescence.

However, the young person experiencing many or all of the symptoms on an ongoing basis may be suffering from a deeper form of depression. They may find that these feelings of sadness and despair are harder to shake off. This increased intensity of depression may result from the following factors:

- Being bullied at school, feeling unwanted, ridiculed, dismissed, or excluded. Not having friends at school to talk to, to share school breaks with, to walk home with. Equally, not having friends outside of school, and not being part of any group.
- Believing that adults will not, or cannot, rescue you if you are being bullied, and living a life of fear, shame, and intimidation.
- Experiencing rejection, such as not being picked for the soccer team, not getting an invitation to parties, being left alone at discos, and being shunned when trying to make friends.
- Not wanting to go home because you are fighting with your parents or your parents are fighting with each other. Wishing your home was happier, like your friends' homes seem to be.
- Experiencing deep despair at losing a boyfriend or girlfriend. Believing that because the relationship is over that you are unloved or unlovable. This may include crying, playing sad music, waiting for the telephone to ring, and thinking your world has come to an end.
- Having your world turned upside down by your parents separating or divorcing, or threatening to do so. Wondering how you will cope, where you will live, who you will live with. Feeling angry, rejected, betrayed, and experiencing grief.
- Suffering the death of a family member or a close friend. Finding this grief hard to cope with, and not knowing where to seek help.
- Experiencing adults as insensitive, uncaring, lacking in understanding, or unsupportive. Feeling that you are not liked by your parents, and wondering if they love you at all.

- Becoming distressed as a result of a parental alcohol problem. Being embarrassed, upset, or fearful of their behaviour towards you when they drink. Sometimes, experiencing, or worrying about, violence in your home.
- Being worried about your parents' health, having a parent who is ill and in hospital, wondering if they will survive or die.
- Experiencing physical, verbal or sexual abuse. Recognition of the impact and significance of such abuse can be disturbing to the adolescent.
- Envying a brother or sister who appears to be more attractive, more intelligent, more accomplished. Secretly believing that your parents love you less than other family members.
- Having physical complaints, being ill, feeling unwell, feeling less healthy than your peers.
- Experiencing difficulty going to sleep. Waking up feeling unrefreshed and anxious. Waking up early, and being unable to return to sleep. Dreading the coming day.
- Experiencing peer pressure over sexual behaviour, alcohol, and drugs. Not knowing how to disengage from delinquent acts.
- Worrying that you may be pregnant, or worrying that you may have caused someone else to become pregnant. Wondering what to do, fearing that nobody may help, and dreading the reaction of parents.
- Being anxious about social situations, not knowing what to do or say, worrying about fainting or nausea, and believing that you will be humiliated in the company of others.
- Being afraid to go to school (phobia), or being afraid that something may happen to your parents or family in your absence at school (separation anxiety).
- Failing an important examination such as the Leaving Certificate or other Third Level examination. As a result, experi-

encing intense fears for the future.

At this stage, the intensity, frequency, and duration of the sadness and despair have increased. There is a feeling that everything is out of control, and a significant darkness has entered the life of the adolescent. The adolescent's life has become distressing and miserable. Their unhappiness is such that the depression has taken hold of their life, and the danger now exists that they may contemplate ending it all.

The adolescent may now be experiencing the following dominant and persistent moods:

- Prolonged grief is experienced at the losses in life. Grief and mourning are now predominant.
- There is an increased inability to recover from any shock or shame caused by events such as examination failure.
- It becomes increasingly difficult, if not impossible, to lift the clouds of depression. The adolescent begins not to care anymore, to see no future, and to feel helpless and hopeless about life.
- Fragile self-esteem has been shattered, and feelings of self-loathing, shame and worthlessness are emerging.
- A sense of defeat and pessimism has set in. The adolescent begins to think that death may provide a release, and wonders how to achieve this.
- Mourning takes place for the security of childhood identity, and the prospect of an adult identity seems unattainable.
- Prevalent feelings include a sense of emptiness, of being surrounded by shadows, finding that life is passing by in slow motion.
- The conclusion is reached that nothing can help you, and that nobody cares enough to try to rescue you.

- Suicide may be considered as a solution to pain and suffering, and the adolescent wonders about the reactions of others in the event of suicide.

SUICIDE

Sadly, suicide has become one of the major causes of death among young people. Both suicide and attempted suicide rates increase from puberty onwards, and the incidence of both is high in Ireland.

Studies show that being depressed raises the risk of dying by suicide by approximately 500%, and it would be fair to suggest that there is a strong relationship between suicide and depression. We, therefore, need to be specially vigilant when young people are unhappy, upset or depressed, in order to avoid the tragic and unnecessary severing of life through suicide.

We can easily be seduced into dismissing adolescent threats of suicide as the dramatic gestures of adolescent excess. However, studies show that the majority of those who commit suicide have made threats beforehand (most of those who make such attempts are girls; most of those who succeed are boys). Therefore, although attempted suicide may well be a cry for help, it is tragically a cry that is often not heard on time.

RECOGNISING SIGNS OF SUICIDAL INTENT

If there is the slightest possibility that your adolescent has reached a stage of depression where they may end their life, seek *immediate* psychiatric attention. The signs that a young person may be contemplating such an act are as follows:

- Indicating that the family would be better off if the adolescent were elsewhere. This may be accompanied by suicide threats or expressions of a wish to die. Poor communication between the adolescent and parents can add to the problems at this time.

- Becoming increasingly withdrawn, isolated, lonely, having no friends, or no observable success at school, at home, in relationships, or in life in general.
- Exhibiting depression, particularly if prolonged, intense, and unshakeable. There may be accompanying eating and sleeping disturbances, declining school progress, and deterioration in relationships with others.
- Asking questions about how a parent would feel if the adolescent died. Seeking the parent's views on life after death, on the morality of suicide, or on the parent's general reactions to the concept of suicide.
- Tidying up rooms, sorting out personal belongings, in particular giving away favourite possessions.
- Asking a parent or brothers and sisters if they would look after a pet in the event of anything happening to the adolescent.
- Contacting old friends, relations, visiting grandparents, or any unexpected resurgence of interest in others. This may be the parting contact or final visit.
- Giving an unexpected hug to parents, saying something loving, and being especially attentive to younger brothers and sisters. If this is out of character, it may be the adolescent's way of saying 'goodbye'.
- Expressing intense and emotional 'goodbyes' when parents are going out or when the adolescent is leaving the house. Making an unexpected gesture of affection or love at this time.

The threat of suicide in adolescence should never be underestimated by parents. Not alone is it one of the major causes of death in young people, but it is also growing at a rapid rate.

It is informative to note that 80% of those who attempt

suicide have discussed their intentions with others. It is equally worthwhile for parents to be aware that adolescents planning suicide will invariably leave clues as to their intentions.

From this it follows that a careful scrutiny of the adolescent's moods and performance, behavioural patterns, and reactions to pressure can do much to minimise the risk.

DISCIPLINE

ADOLESCENCE IS A TIME WHEN young people are experimenting, discovering, challenging, testing limits, and pushing and extending boundaries. However, adolescence is also a time when young people are most at risk of making ill-considered or dangerous decisions, particularly during the earlier adolescent years.

The consequences of making unwise decisions can be severe, and can influence the adolescent's future life. Behaviours such as school truancy, academic neglect, drug taking, excessive alcohol intake, premature sexual activity, drunken driving, and committing delinquent acts can interrupt and arrest the adolescent's progress towards mature and responsible adulthood.

Therefore, the teenage years are the time when parents need to draw clear boundaries about what is acceptable and useful behaviour and what is unacceptable and dangerous. This involves a difficult and delicate balancing act between, on the one hand, guiding and limiting the behaviour of adolescents and, on the other hand, allowing the adolescent the space and freedom to grow up.

To accommodate this dilemma, most parents introduce a form of discipline lying somewhere between the parameters of safety and autonomy; between keeping adolescents safe during the teenage years and allowing the growing development of independence and self-control. Discipline, within such constraints, usually operates well for both adolescent and adult.

The period of adolescence, for both parents and teenagers, is not dissimilar to learning to drive. The adolescent who drives too quickly before knowing how a car operates, what the rules of the road are, how to deal with oncoming vehicles, how to steer steadily rather than wildly from one side to the other, and how to apply the brakes, is in serious danger.

Equally, the parent who attempts to teach the adolescent to drive by anticipating the dangers around every corner, by controlling the steering wheel, the gears and the brakes, has not taught the adolescent to drive. A steady speed, constantly observing ahead, with gentle guidance of the steering wheel, and soft application of the brakes when necessary, guarantees a smoother journey.

Discipline, during the teenage years, also needs to be gentle, firm, consistent, with a gradual reduction in parental control as the adolescent becomes more competent at steering a safe course into adulthood and beyond.

Most young people want rules and boundaries that are fair, consistent and firmly implemented. Having boundaries reassures them that they are being kept safe by people who love them. When the adolescent crosses those boundaries, prompts or cues are required to call the young person back from potential danger.

Equally, rewards are the mechanisms by which we encourage young people to stay within defined behavioural boundaries. The drawing and enforcing of boundaries is often referred to as 'discipline' and 'punishment'.

SYMPTOMS OF A BREAKDOWN IN DISCIPLINE
It is estimated that between 15–20% of adolescents may experienced prolonged and intense conflict with parents over issues of discipline. When behaviour is difficult, defiant, aggressive, uncontrolled, or uncontrollable, parents are understandably confused and upset, and ask, 'Where did we go wrong?'

Discipline may break down for many reasons. The following are some reasons why discipline may become an issue between adolescents and their parents:

173

- The discipline is incomprehensible to the young person, who does not understand what is required.
- It has been imposed without any rationale, logic, or apparent explanation.
- The discipline is too punitive and harsh. The adolescent is hurt, humiliated and angry, and reacts against it by producing behaviour that is challenging, dangerous, retaliatory, or designed to shock.
- The discipline is too lax, and the young person has received little guidance as to what is required of them. The adolescent is uncertain about which boundaries are important and which are not.
- The discipline is confused, and one parent imposes greater discipline than the other.
- The discipline is contradictory. For example, the adolescent is rewarded at home for a behaviour, such as taking an initiative or asking a question, that is punished at school.
- There are gross differences between the restrictions imposed on the adolescent and on the adolescent's peers. For example, the peers are allowed to engage in many activities that the adolescent is not allowed to engage in.
- The discipline is inconsistent. In other words, behaviour that is rewarded one day is punished the next. In the confusion, adolescents must rely on their own judgement, rather than be subject to the vicissitudes of parental control.
- The discipline is non-existent, and the young person has no sense of direction and no boundaries to guide their behaviour.
- The discipline is ambivalent. One or both parents may have mixed or ambivalent feelings about wanting the adolescent to grow up while also wishing that the young person would remain dependent. This is particularly confusing for adolescents.

174

WHY DISCIPLINE IS A GOOD IDEA

Adolescents whose parents do not make rules perceive their parents as behaving in an 'indifferent' fashion. Indeed, teenagers without rules often go to extreme lengths to energise or worry their parents so that rules are created. This is partly because adolescents need, and look for, guidance. Discipline also achieves the following:

- Establishes rules of behaviour that accord with the norm.
- Generates self-confidence that arises from knowing what is expected and being able to achieve it.
- Acts as a sign that parents are interested and concerned.
- Allows the adolescent to take on the responsibilities of growing up in a graded and appropriate way.
- Establishes clear boundaries, thereby helping to avoid conflict and confrontation within the family and elsewhere.
- Establishes a routine to be followed.
- Helps avoid the consequences of getting into trouble with friends at school, or with the Gardaí.
- Fosters academic success, through encouraging a disciplined pattern of study.
- Prepares adolescents for conforming to rules in later life, e.g., at work and in society in general.
- Helps maintain safety, which is especially important at a time of widespread availability of drugs and alcohol.
- Fosters an understanding of social skills, including tidiness at home and learning how to live with others.
- Helps establish a healthy lifestyle and healthy eating habits.
- Sets rules regarding sexual promiscuity, thereby avoiding unwanted pregnancies.

Adolescents experience physical punishment as humiliating, hurtful and unacceptable, and in one Irish survey of 12–15 year olds, over 90% of those who responded considered physical punishment to be unacceptable.

Furthermore, a young person who has been curtailed, controlled and excessively disciplined is unlikely to be able to develop independence in thinking, or to make mature and independent choices. Opportunities for learning are restricted if behaviour is delineated and no allowances are made for individual circumstances or choice. When such discipline is imposed, the adolescent may retreat into compliant, depressed, or apathetic behaviour which is designed to avoid the sanctions of the parent.

Alternatively, adolescents may respond to a pattern of harsh and physically punitive discipline by engaging in equally aggressive, unsympathetic, or bullying behaviour outside the home. Indeed, it has been found that the more criticism and physical punishment a young person receives, the higher are the chances that they will become emotionally disturbed and engage in anti-social or delinquent behaviour.

The following points are of note:

- Research shows that physical punishment is the least effective form of discipline.
- Physical punishment teaches that 'might is right'.
- Physical punishment models violent and aggressive behaviour, and does not teach about control over emotions.
- Physical assault or punishment antagonises and angers many adolescents, who may subsequently enact their anger and distress in aggressive behaviour towards the next weaker person.
- There is a strong link between delinquent behaviour and

being a victim of extremely physical, inconsistent, or punitive discipline.

- Adolescents become understandably confused when physically punished for their own acts of physical violence. This sends contradictory messages to the adolescent.
- The task of establishing an individual identity in adolescence is disrupted if discipline does not allow the development of one's own choices and 'sense of self'.

Different rules of discipline for different ages

While the term 'adolescence' is a generic term, designed to cover the period between childhood and adulthood, adolescence itself covers at least three distinct stages: *early* adolescence, *middle* adolescence and *late* adolescence.

Obviously, the rules and discipline for 11–12 year olds will differ radically from those which apply to the late teens. Furthermore, depending on the maturity, intelligence, street wisdom, truthfulness and stability of the young person, in addition to the safety of their surrounding environment, you may wish to apply different rules.

Early adolescence – This early stage spans the time from puberty, or approximately 11–13 years, up to approximately 14–16 years of age. During this adolescent stage, young people are most at risk from peer pressure. This is also the time when the physiological changes are most dramatic and abrupt, and it brings the beginning of interest in members of the opposite sex.

Additionally, this stage usually coincides with the transition into Secondary School, and with all the social and academic adjustments required of the adolescent during this transition. This is the time when clear, firm and consistently enforced rules are required to help establish understanding and trust between adolescents and parents.

A parent has the right to know where the young adolescent

177

is, with whom they are spending their time, and how they are getting home. The parent is also entitled to collect the teenager to ensure their safety. Equally, parents should set a specific time limit after which the young person must be indoors. This is a time when conflict is likely, but most young people secretly welcome the security of parental rules while they themselves push for independence.

Middle Adolescence – This middle period spans the stage from approximately 15–17 years. This is a time when the first drama of adolescence has subsided, and adolescents may well be making individual friendships with the opposite sex, taking state examinations, learning to drive a car, and seeking further independence in managing their time, their friendships, and their study.

Parents should still request information on the adolescent's itinerary, and have the right to know where the young person is and with whom they are spending their time. However, they should allow the adolescent to come in at a later hour and to take more responsibility for their own welfare, such as personal care, school attendance, and study. Parents should increasingly help the young person to weigh up the pros and cons of a situation by providing background guidance and support.

Late Adolescence – This covers the age period from approximately 16–19 years, and encompasses the shift from juvenile to adult status, the acquiring of legal permission to drink alcohol, to vote, and to drive a car. Vocational choice will probably be decided during these years, and the adolescent may have left school to pursue further study or their career choice. At this stage, a parent's role should be supportive, caring, and advisory.

WHAT SHOULD PARENTS DO?

- Decide on a schedule for room tidying, house cleaning and other domestic chores, that involves regular contributions from the adolescent.

- Don't decide on rules or impose punishment on a whim. Rules must be thought out, consistent, and applied over time, not thought up on the spur of the moment.

- Relate punishments to specific offences, and explain why they are being imposed.

- Make the consequences of a breach of discipline clear in advance. In this way, the adolescent has a choice to adhere to the rule or disobey it.

- Make sure you are not punishing the adolescent to compensate for your own moods, frustrations, or depressions.

- Explain the reason for rules. For example, it might be wise to use phrases such as, 'This is for your safety and protection'.

- Rules should be set with a purpose. They should not be restrictions for the sake of wielding parental power.

- Try not to force adolescents 'into a corner'. At the adolescent stage of life, 'backing down' is a real problem.

- Don't back yourself into a corner. Issuing an ultimatum can be difficult and dangerous, particularly if it suggests that the young person ought to leave the house if they don't conform.

- Choose battles carefully, and avoid the trivial and petty.

- Stand firm over your decisions regarding rules. Don't let the adolescent see that nagging or pleading will force you to change your mind.

- To avoid confusion, ensure that discipline at home and at school are synchronised. Don't expect the school to do the disciplining for you.

- Choose a school that has a discipline pattern consistent

with your own.

- Try not to use payments or bribes to get your adolescent to conform.
- Ensure that rules are fair and consistent, and applied to all adolescents in the family (allowance must be made for the age of the adolescent).
- Safety and the adolescent's well-being should be the key concerns in deciding what rules to impose.
- Don't discipline an adolescent in front of their friends, thereby causing shame and embarrassment.
- Being constantly critical or sarcastic to the adolescent is not an appropriate approach. It will merely shatter their self-esteem.
- If you must criticise, criticise the behaviour, not the person.
- Avoid using phrases such as, 'Don't ever let me catch you drinking'. This challenges the adolescent to drink and not be caught.
- Assert your right to draw boundaries, establish times that the young person must come home, places that they may and may not go to, influences that they may or may not be exposed to.
- Be clear about what is allowed and what is forbidden. Do not deviate on important behaviours and values, whatever the pressure. However, be informed about what is appropriate for the adolescent in terms of clothes, mixing with friends, times to come home, etc.
- Try to avoid 'double-binding' or confusing commands that are impossible to comply with, e.g., saying, 'Act your age, act like a grown up'. An adolescent is not yet ready to be an adult.
- Never hit a young person. This only teaches violence, is humiliating, and is an abuse of power. Remember that they may go on to respond to others by using physical intimi-

dation.

- Don't be afraid to act like a parent. Don't try to act like, or to look like, your teenager. Adolescents need parents.
- Always remember that a parent's model of behaviour is the most influential and powerful model on display, and that young people will often repeat what they observe. However, also remember that there may be other contradictory models in society, in the media, and in the behaviour of others.
- If adolescents have lost control of their behaviour, their social conduct, their emotions, or even their mental health, attention is required. Do not be afraid to seek professional help. It is not a reflection on your parenting, but is rather a mark of your concern.
- Don't overprotect the adolescent. They need to make friends, learn to be independent, and make safe mistakes in order to learn, and they need to learn to survive. Eventually, they will need to be able to survive without you.
- Never abandon the adolescent. If they are immature enough to make gross mistakes, or vulnerable enough to experience emotional disturbance, they are certainly not able to 'go it alone'.
- Never stop nurturing the young person's self-esteem. High self-esteem is one of the greatest protectors from behavioural or emotional disturbance.

The tasks of adolescence are many. Whether a young person accomplishes these tasks or fails to do so depends primarily on their relationship with their parents. Indeed, it is important that parents do not underestimate the critical role they play in the social, emotional, intellectual, spiritual and psychological development of the young person during the teenage years.

At all times, the dignity, integrity and self-esteem of the individual must be respected. In many ways, this brings us back to where we began this book, namely that all the rules and structures must be devised to allow the adolescent to grow, to develop physically, intellectually and emotionally, and to flourish and develop the confidence and personality to tackle problems in later life. This is a time when the adolescent's self-esteem needs to be fostered and nourished. It is only with a proper 'sense of self' that they can tackle the problems of the future with confidence.

Other Interesting Books

NERVOUS BREAKDOWN
Edited by COLM KEANE

The number one Irish bestseller on psychological distress – includes chapters on depression, addiction, phobias, obsessions, bereavement, panic, eating and sleeping disorders, and offers advice on how to cope with the pressures and stresses of everyday life.

'Makes understandable the whole span of mental anguish ... Buy the book'. *Evening Echo*

'Excellent'. *Irish Press*

'Deals with each topic in a very easy to read manner and it offers practical information and advice'. *Gay Byrne, RTE Radio 1*

'Highly informative and very easily read'. *Cork Examiner*

'Marvellous compendium of skills and advice'. *Dr Patrick Murray, Chairman, Southern Health Board*

'I honestly think everyone should read this book'. *Biddy White-Lennon, RTE Radio 1*

Maximum Points – Minimum Panic
The Essential Guide to Surviving Exams
Kevin Flanagan

The pressure to succeed is enormous and still growing. Here is a guide that will give students the tools not only to survive but to excel in exams.

The approach is two-fold – practical, easy to follow tips that assist and promote learning while encouraging relaxation and quality time out.

'I would highly recommend it for helping students to deal with the stress of exams.' *Fr Simon Sleeman, Principal, Glenstal Abbey School*

'Extremely useful in helping students find a path through the maze that is our exam system.' *Brian Mooney, Lecturer in Postgraduate Education, UCD*

'Contains really useful information ... Its approach is holistic and realistic – I would recommend it.' *Patrick O'Mahony, Principal, Newbridge College*

'He's good at giving advice about how to timetable learning, how to revise and how to avoid distractions ... I have no doubt that this book would galvanise some youngsters into action.' *Biddy White-Lennon, RTE*

MARIE MURRAY is Principal Clinical Psychologist and Head of the Psychology Department at St Vincent's Psychiatric Hospital, Dublin, and St Joseph's Adolescent Services, Dublin. She is a graduate of University College, Dublin, where she is currently a Senior Tutor. She also lectures at UCD, Dublin City University and the Mater Misericordiae Hospital, Dublin.

COLM KEANE is a Senior Producer with RTE Radio 1, where he won a Jacobs' Award and a Glaxo Fellowship for European Science Writers. He is a graduate of Trinity College, Dublin and Georgetown University, Washington DC. Since 1991, he has published six books, including the bestsellers *The Jobs Crisis, Nervous Breakdown, Death and Dying* and *The Stress File*.